Strategies for Test-Taking Success:
Math

Christy M. Newman
Judith Diamond

THOMSON
™
HEINLE

Australia • Canada • Mexico • Singapore • Spain • United Kingdom • United States

THOMSON

HEINLE

Strategies for Test-Taking Success: Math
Christy M. Newman / Judith Diamond

Publisher: *Phyllis Dobbins*
Director of Product Development: *Anita Raducanu*
Director, ELL Training and Development: *Evelyn Nelson*
Director of Product Marketing: *Amy Mabley*
Product Marketing Manager: *Laura Needham*
Sr. Field Marketing Manager: *Robert Walters*
Associate Development Editor: *John Hicks*

Editorial Assistant: *Lindsey Musen*
Production Editor: *Chrystie Hopkins*
Manufacturing Manager: *Marcia Locke*
Development Editor: *Weston Editorial*
Design and Production Services: *Pre-Press Company, Inc.*
Cover Designer: *Studio Montage*
Printer: *Banta Book Group*

For permission to use material from this text or product, submit
a request online at http://www.thomsonrights.com

Any additional questions about permissions can be submitted
by email to thomsonrights@thomson.com

ISBN: 1-4130-0925-5
      1-4130-1548-4 (International Student Edition)

Library of Congress Control Number:
2005925887

For more information contact Thomson Heinle, 25
Thomson Place, Boston, Massachusetts 02210 USA, or you
can visit our Internet site at elt.thomson.com

Table of Contents

CHAPTER 1   **Introduction**   1

Math Pretest   1

    Strategy 1   Make a Long-Term Study Plan   13

    Strategy 2   Learn about Question Types and Test-Taking Strategies   15

CHAPTER 2   **Whole Numbers and Number Sense**   19

    Strategy 3   Addition and Subtraction   19

    Strategy 4   Understand Place Value   25

    Strategy 5   Add and Subtract Large Numbers   28

    Strategy 6   Multiplication and Division   32

    Strategy 7   Multiply Large Numbers   36

    Strategy 8   Divide Larger Numbers   41

Chapter 2 Review Test   45

CHAPTER 3   **Fractions, Decimals, and Percents**   49

    Strategy 9   Describe Fractions   49

    Strategy 10   Add and Subtract Fractions with the Same Denominator   52

    Strategy 11   Multiply Fractions   54

    Strategy 12   Add and Subtract Fractions with Different Denominators   58

    Strategy 13   Divide and Simplify Fractions   60

    Strategy 14   Compare Decimals and Fractions   63

    Strategy 15   Add and Subtract Decimals   65

    Strategy 16   Multiply and Divide Decimals   67

    Strategy 17   Percents   70

Chapter 3 Review Test   75

CHAPTER 4   **Algebra**   79

    Strategy 18   Work with Positive and Negative Numbers   79

    Strategy 19   Add and Subtract with Variables   84

    Strategy 20   Multiply and Divide with Variables   87

    Strategy 21   Solve Algebra Problems   89

    Strategy 22   Inequalities   93

    Strategy 23   Try Different Strategies to Solve Problems   95

Chapter 4 Review Test   99

CHAPTER 5   **Probability, Data, and Statistics**   **103**

    Strategy 24   Ratios   **103**

    Strategy 25   Probability   **107**

    Strategy 26   Graphs   **109**

    Strategy 27   Equations of a Line   **114**

    Strategy 28   Mean, Median, Mode   **118**

Chapter 5 Review Test   **121**

CHAPTER 6   **Geometry**   **127**

    Strategy 29   Shapes   **127**

    Strategy 30   Circumference and Perimeter   **132**

    Strategy 31   Area   **137**

    Strategy 32   Volume   **143**

    Strategy 33   Pythagorean Theorem   **146**

    Strategy 34   Rotation, Reflection, and Translation   **149**

Chapter 6 Review Test   **151**

CHAPTER 7   **Put It All Together**   **155**

Cumulative Practice Test 1   **159**

Cumulative Practice Test 2   **173**

CHAPTER 8   **Get the Best Score**   **185**

GLOSSARY   **187**

GLOSARIO (Spanish Glossary)   **189**

INDEX   **191**

REPRODUCIBLE ANSWER GRID   **193**

ANSWER KEY   **195**

Acknowledgments

I wish to thank Phyllis Dobbins and Anita Raducanu—for all their friendship and encouragement during the creation of *Strategies for Test-Taking Success*. Thanks, too, to Evelyn Nelson for her amazing ideas.

I'd also like to thank the following people at Thomson ELT: John Hicks, Katherine Reilly, and Chrystie Hopkins, for their professionalism, creativity, and commitment to this project.

Thanks also to Tom Friedman, my partner at Weston Editorial, with his unflagging support, energy, and vision and my children, Corey and Jonathan.

Christy M. Newman

I would like to thank all the hardworking people at Thomson ELT for their conception, encouragement, and support for this project.

I would especially like to thank Christy Newman for her clear vision, kind words and the ability to say no so nicely. Thanks also to Jonathan Friedman for a perspective on the math problems from someone who has so recently "been there and done that." Finally, a last thank you to all those students, adults, and teenagers, whose "Why?" made me learn to think hard and explain better.

Judith Diamond

The authors and publisher would also like to thank the following reviewers:

Yuri Gonzalez
Rialto High School
Rialto, CA

Lisa Troute
School District of Palm Beach County
Palm Beach, FL

Graciela Morales
Austin Independent School District
Austin, TX

Cally Williams
Newcomers High School
Long Island City, NY

Mona Piñon
Oxnard Union High School District
Oxnard, CA

Darlene York
California State University, Chico
Chico, CA

About This Book

STRATEGIES FOR TEST-TAKING SUCCESS is a test preparation series designed to help all students develop effective test-taking skills and strategies. The series uses clear, easy-to-understand language and examples, with illustrations and activities. It provides support for foundation skills. It also teaches and practices advanced skills and concepts in an easy, accessible way. The series incorporates scientifically based research in the areas of reading, math, and writing.

Features

- The **instructional chapters** focus on major skills and standards concepts tested in most standardized state tests. Each chapter is divided into short lessons, called **Strategies**. Each Strategy focuses on a discrete skill or concept. The techniques rely on proven test-taking strategies.

- **Clear, simple language** and **illustrations** support higher-order thinking skills.

- The **Pretest** helps evaluate current skills. Areas-of-need are recorded on a **Skills Chart.**

- **Keys To Understanding** highlight key words, questions, and/or special test-taking pointers to learn.

- **Tips** offer practical aids and hints.

- **Practice Questions** review skills and concepts taught in the lesson. They progress from controlled to productive and open-ended questions.

- The **Review Tests** and two **Cumulative Tests** simulate the format, length, and language of authentic standardized tests. Questions ask about newly taught material and recycle what was taught earlier.

- The **Answer Key** thoroughly explains both correct and incorrect answer choices.

- The reproducible **Answer Grid** is used to practice filling in "bubble sheets" for standardized tests.

- English and Spanish **Glossaries** define key terms.

- ExamView Pro® software allows for test item customization, re-testing, and computer-delivered practice.

How to Use This Book

Students can use this book to study and review for standardized state tests. This book helps students understand what a standardized test is like. They learn the best ways to take standardized tests and practice taking them.

Teachers can use this book as a "reteach and reassess" tool to target specific standards-based skills and concepts where additional practice is needed. It can also be used for whole-class instruction or as an individual tutorial.

References

Drijvers, P.H.M. *Classroom-based Research in Mathematics Education.* Utrecht, the Netherlands: Freudenthal Institute, 2004.

Lamon, Susan J. "Beyond constructivism: An improved fitness metaphor for the acquisition of mathematical knowledge," in *Beyond Constructivism: A Model and Modeling Perspective On Problem Solving, Learning, and Instruction in Mathematics,* R. Lesh & H.M. Doerr (eds) Mahwah, NJ: Lawrence Erlbaum Associates, 2003.

Principles and Standards for School Mathematics. Reston, VA: National Council of Teachers of Mathematics, 2000.

Spielberger, C.D. "Conceptual and methodological issues in anxiety research," in *Anxiety: Current Trends in Theory and Research,* Spielberger, C.D. (ed), New York: Academic Press, 1972.

Spielberger, C.D. *Manual for the State-Trait Anxiety Inventory Form.* Palo Alto, CA: Consulting Psychologists Press, 1983.

Introduction

Math Pretest

The Math Pretest tells you two important things:

- **What you know.** The Math Pretest shows the math skills you have now. Review those skills or start to learn and practice new ones.

- **What you need to learn.** The Math Pretest shows the new math skills you need to learn and practice.

Directions: The Math Pretest has 24 questions. There are questions about whole numbers, fractions, decimals, statistics, algebra, and geometry.

1. Read each question carefully.

2. Look at any charts, tables, or graphs.

3. Answer the questions. Pick only *one* answer for each question.

4. Mark your answer on the Answer Grid.

EXAMPLE:
17. (A) (B) ● (D)

ANSWER GRID

1. (A) (B) (C) (D)	9. (A) (B) (C) (D)	17. (A) (B) (C) (D)
2. (A) (B) (C) (D)	10. (A) (B) (C) (D)	18. (A) (B) (C) (D)
3. (A) (B) (C) (D)	11. (A) (B) (C) (D)	19. (A) (B) (C) (D)
4. (A) (B) (C) (D)	12. (A) (B) (C) (D)	20. (A) (B) (C) (D)
5. (A) (B) (C) (D)	13. (A) (B) (C) (D)	21. (A) (B) (C) (D)
6. (A) (B) (C) (D)	14. (A) (B) (C) (D)	22. (A) (B) (C) (D)
7. (A) (B) (C) (D)	15. (A) (B) (C) (D)	23. (A) (B) (C) (D)
8. (A) (B) (C) (D)	16. (A) (B) (C) (D)	24. (A) (B) (C) (D)

MATH PRETEST

1 This is Carol's shopping list for school clothes: 3 pairs of jeans, 2 sweaters, and a pair of shoes. The jeans are $20.00 each. One sweater costs $35.00. The other sweater costs $29.00. The shoes are $38.00. How much money does Carol need?

A $112.00

B $122.00

C $162.00

D $168.00

2 Juan sees a lion walk around its cage. The cage is 7 feet wide and 8 feet long. The lion walks around the perimeter of its cage 15 times every half hour. Juan wonders how far it walks in 12 hours.

A 450 feet

B 2640 feet

C 5400 feet

D 10800 feet

3 Shauna, Ling, and Erica have CD collections. Ling has 5 more CDs than Shauna. Shauna has three times as many as Erica. Ling has 20 CDs. How many does Erica have?

A 3

B 5

C 20

D 60

4 Luis thinks he rides his bike 35 miles an hour. In 15 minutes, he rides 8 miles. How fast does Luis really ride?

A 8 miles an hour

B 23 miles an hour

C 32 miles an hour

D 40 miles an hour

GO ON

5 Sonja is at a fast-food restaurant. She wants to eat fewer than 1000 calories. Look at the table. Which meal can she eat?

Food	Calories
cheeseburger	330
jumbo cheeseburger	530
small fries	257
medium fries	356
large fries	514
small shake	620
medium shake	790
cola	80

A   jumbo cheeseburger, large fries, cola

B   jumbo cheeseburger, small fries, small shake

C   cheeseburger, large fries, medium shake

D   jumbo cheeseburger, small fries, cola

6 This is Lee's record of rainfall for six months.

Month	Rainfall
July	0.75 inch
August	0.09 inch
September	3.97 inches
October	2.08 inches
November	2.10 inches
December	1.48 inches

Lee uses this data to list the months from the wettest to the driest. Which list is correct?

A   August, September, July, December, October, November

B   September, October, November, December, August, July

C   August, July, December, October, November, September

D   September, November, October, December, July, August

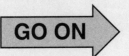

GO ON

7 Eleni makes 2 chocolate pudding pies. She needs a crumb crust for each pie. She doubles her recipe. What amounts does she use in the new recipe?

Eleni's Crumb Crust Recipe
$1\frac{1}{2}$ cups ground vanilla wafers
5 tablespoons butter
$\frac{1}{3}$ cup sugar
$\frac{3}{4}$ teaspoon salt

A 3 cups vanilla wafers, 10 tablespoons butter, $\frac{2}{3}$ cup sugar, $1\frac{1}{2}$ teaspoons salt

B $2\frac{1}{2}$ cups vanilla wafers, 10 tablespoons butter, $\frac{2}{3}$ cup sugar, 1 teaspoon salt

C $\frac{3}{2}$ cup vanilla wafers, 10 tablespoons butter, $\frac{1}{6}$ cup sugar, $\frac{3}{8}$ teaspoon salt

D $2\frac{2}{4}$ cups vanilla wafers, 10 tablespoons butter, $\frac{2}{6}$ cup sugar, $\frac{6}{8}$ teaspoon salt

8 Alexandra and José work at an ice cream shop. They look at the chart below. It shows the most popular flavors sold on July 17th. On July 18th, Alexandra and José plan to buy 2 tubs of vanilla, 2 tubs of mint chocolate chip, and 2 tubs of butter pecan. Which plan is better?

Ice Cream Sold on July 17th	Sales
vanilla	30%
mint chocolate chip	10%
butter pecan	5%

A Buy more chocolate chip and butter pecan. Alexandra and José have less of those flavors.

B Keep data for more than one day. Then decide.

C Don't buy more vanilla. It is not a fancy flavor.

D Buy more chocolate. Most people like chocolate best.

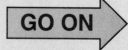

9 Hector takes a survey. He asks what kind of car people like to drive. He asks 50 people. This table shows the results.

Type of Car	SUV	Compact Car	Luxury Car	Sports Car
Number of People	16	9	7	18

Look at the circle graphs. Which one shows the percentage of people who like each type of car?

A

Car Choices

6
5
11
14

Key
- SUV
- Compact Car
- Luxury Car
- Sports Car

B

Car Choices

16
18
9
7

Key
- SUV
- Compact Car
- Luxury Car
- Sports Car

C

Car Choices

18
7
16
9

Key
- SUV
- Compact Car
- Luxury Car
- Sports Car

D

Car Choices

84
82
91
93

Key
- SUV
- Compact Car
- Luxury Car
- Sports Car

10 What situation does this expression represent: $x + \frac{1}{2}x = y$

  A   Add 50% to the total price.

  B   Take 50% off the total price.

  C   Buy 2 and get the second one free.

  D   Buy 2 and get the second one half off.

11 Greg looks for a digital camera on the Internet. He finds 5 cameras. They cost $325.00, $339.00, $367.00, $367.00, and $384.00. What is the mean price for the cameras?

  A $339.00

  B $356.40

  C $367.00

  D $384.00

12 Tuen has a sports catalog. Everything in the catalog is 33% off the regular price. Shipping costs are $2.75. What formula can he use to figure out the cost of anything in the catalog?

  A $2.75x + .33$

  B $2.75x + .67$

  C $.33x - 2.75$

  D $.67x + 2.75$

13 Marina runs a 5-kilometer race. She can run a mile in 8.5 minutes. 1 mile = .62 kilometers How fast can Marina run the race?

  A   24.80 minutes

  B   25.50 minutes

  C   26.35 minutes

  D   42.50 minutes

GO ON

Strategies for Test-Taking Success: Math © Thomson Heinle. Photocopying this page is prohibited by law.

14 **What is the relationship between a cat's speed and its weight?**

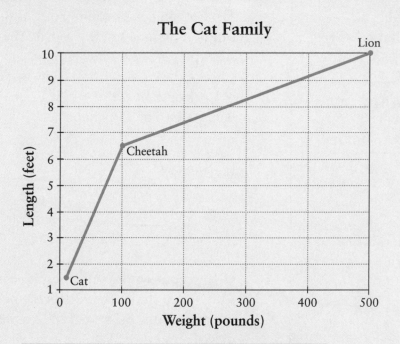

The Cat Family

Type of Cat	Running Speed in Miles per Hour
house cat	30
cheetah	70
lion	50

A The less a cat weighs, the faster it runs.

B The more a cat weighs, the faster it runs.

C The ratio between a cat's weight and its length is one reason it runs so fast.

D There is no clear relationship between a cat's weight and how fast it runs.

15 Jerry is late for school. He grabs a piece of fruit from a bowl. The pieces of fruit are listed in the table below. What is the probability that he will grab an orange?

CONTENTS OF THE FRUIT BOWL	
Fruit	**Number**
oranges	4
pears	3
bananas	3
apples	5

A $\frac{1}{15}$

B $\frac{4}{15}$

C $\frac{1}{4}$

D $\frac{11}{15}$

16 You have to be ≥ 39 inches and ≤ 55 inches tall to go on the Junior Roller Coaster at the amusement park. Gary is 39 inches tall. Maria is 42 inches tall. Mansoor is 55 inches tall. Joe is 56 inches tall. Who can ride on the Junior Roller Coaster?

A All the children can.

B Only Maria and Joe can.

C Only Gary, Maria, and Mansoor can.

D Only Gary and Mansoor can.

17 Blue whales are the largest mammals in the world. The largest blue whale is 110 feet long. A Thailand bat is the smallest mammal in the world. The smallest bat is 1.14 inches long. Choose the closest estimate of the ratio of the length of a blue whale to the length of a Thailand bat.

A 110 to 1

B 132 to 11

C 1,100 to 114

D 1,300 to 1

18 Olga sees a coat on sale. First it costs $189. Then the store reduces the price by 20%. Later the store reduces the price by another 30%. How much does the coat cost now?

A $83.16

B $94.50

C $105.84

D $139.00

GO ON

Strategies for Test-Taking Success: Math © Thomson Heinle. Photocopying this page is prohibited by law.

19 Somsy has a summer job. He takes care of lawns. A 25-pound bag of grass seed covers 5,000 square feet. Look at the diagram of one lawn. How many bags of grass seed does he need to buy for it?

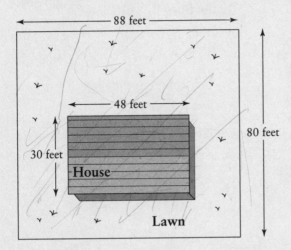

A   1 bag

B   2 bags

C   3 bags

D   4 bags

20 The Dance Committee decorates the gym with balloons. Each bunch of balloons has 3 white ones, 2 blue ones, and 1 red one. The Dance Committee has 120 balloons altogether. How many white balloons do they have?

A   30 white balloons

B   60 white balloons

C   75 white balloons

D   90 white balloons

GO ON

21 Jerry is late for school. He decides to go across the park instead of around it. How far is it across the park?

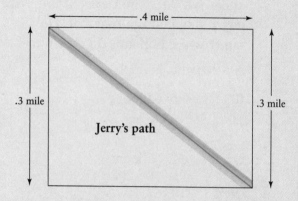

A .1 mile

B .25 mile

C .5 mile

D .7 mile

22 Ryan and Alex go to the same party. The party is 30 miles away. Ryan drives 40 miles an hour. Alex drives 50 miles an hour. Alex gets a flat tire and has to stop for half an hour. Who gets to the party first? How much faster does he get there?

A Ryan gets to the party 21 minutes before Alex.

B Alex gets to the party 11 minutes before Ryan.

C They both get to the party at the same time.

D Alex gets to the party 10 minutes before Ryan.

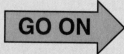

GO ON

Strategies for Test-Taking Success: Math © Thomson Heinle.
Photocopying this page is prohibited by law.

23 Vika wants to know how far it is across the United States. She looks at the scale on a U.S. map. The scale on the map says that 1/2 inch = 600 miles. About how far is it from east to west?

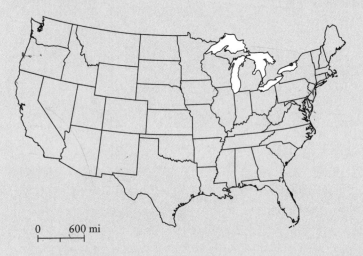

A   600 miles

B   1000 miles

C   2000 miles

D   2800 miles

---

24 Mike has a present to mail. His mother gives him 3 boxes. She thinks they are the same size. He measures them. One box is bigger. Which box holds the most?

Box 1	Box 2	Box 3
5″ × 5″ × 12″	15″ × 9″ × 2.5″	15″ × 9.5″ × 2″

A   All the boxes are equal.

B   Box 1 holds the most.

C   Box 2 holds the most.

D   Box 3 holds the most.

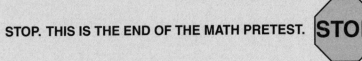

STOP. THIS IS THE END OF THE MATH PRETEST. **STOP**

ANSWER KEY TO THE MATH PRETEST

1. ✓ Check *correct* answers. (Circle) *incorrect* answers.

1. C	7. A	13. C	19. B
2. D	8. B	14. D	20. B
3. B	9. B	15. B	21. C
4. C	10. D	16. C	22. A
5. D	11. B	17. D	23. D
6. D	12. D	18. C	24. C

2. Copy the circled numbers above onto the Skills Chart.

SKILLS CHART

Circle *Incorrect* Answers	Skill Area	Chapter to Study
1, 3, 4, 5	Whole Numbers and Number Sense	Two (page 19)
6, 7, 13, 17, 18	Fractions, Decimals, and Percents	Three (page 49)
8, 9, 11, 12, 14, 15, 22	Algebra	Four (page 79)
10, 16, 20	Probability, Data, and Statistics	Five (page 103)
2, 19, 21, 23, 24	Geometry	Six (page 127)

3. Circle the chapters you need to study. (Hint: You probably need to work on a skill area with two or more incorrect answers.)

Make a Long-Term Study Plan

Strategize for the Test

1. **Before you study:** Think about the "big picture." Think about all the steps on the way to test-taking success. Study and practice your math skills *over time*. Don't wait until the last minute to study. Make studying a *habit*.

2. **Assess your skills:** Look at the Skills Chart on page 12. Are most of your answers correct? Maybe you need to review one chapter. Then 15–20 minutes a day may be enough study time. Or you may need to study several chapters. Then an hour or more a day may be enough time.

3. **Make your plan:** Count your study days between today and the test. Don't count the days when you are busy.

Sun	Mon	Tue	Wed	Thu	Fri	Sat
	1 Today: Make a plan	2 5:00–6 Study time	3 5:00–6 Study time	4 5:00–6 Study time	5 5:00–6 Study time	6 5:00–6 Study time
7 5:00–6 Study time	8 5:00–6 Study time	9 5:00–6 Study time	10 Study for science test	11 5:00–6 Study time	12 5:00–6 Study time	13 5:00–6 Study time
14 5:00–6 Study time	15 5:00–6 Study time	16 5:00–6 Study time	17 5:00–6 Study time	18 5:00–6 Study time	19 Birthday party for Dad	20 5:00–6 Study time
21 5:00–6 Study time	22 5:00–6 Study time	23 5:00–6 Study time	24 5:00–6 Study time	25 5:00–6 Study time	26 5:00–6 Study time	27 School play
28 5:00–6 Study time	29 5:00–6 Study time	30 TEST				

4. **Decide how long you need to study each day:** Write your study time on a calendar or notebook. Check off each day when you finish studying.

5. **Strategize for success:** Keep to your plan. That way you will be prepared. You won't get "stressed out." You won't have to "cram" (study just before the test). Instead, you can relax and get a good night's sleep. You will be ready on the day of the test.

Learn about Question Types and Test-Taking Strategies

It's helpful to know what is on a state math test. This lesson shows you two kinds of questions. It shows you strategies for answering them.

Types of Test Questions

1. **Multiple Choice:** Every test has many multiple-choice questions. (All test questions in *Strategies for Test-Taking Success: Math* are multiple choice.)

A multiple-choice question has two parts: the stem and answer choices. The **stem** can be *an example* or it can *tell a story and ask a question*. There are usually 4 answer choices. You pick the correct *one*.

1 Even numbers can always be—	This stem is part of a sentence.
A divided by 2	
B divided by 3	
C added to make an odd number	The answer choices are A, B, C, or D.
D the product of two odd numbers	
2 Bob throws a ball to Diem. Diem catches it 2 out of every 3 times. Bob throws the ball 18 times. How many times does Diem catch it?	This stem tells a story and asks a question.
A 6	
B 12	
C 18	The answer choices are A, B, C, or D.
D 9	

2. **Open Response:** Some tests have **open-response** questions. You write the answers. Sometimes you have to show your work. You can use the strategies in this book to answer open-response questions too.

To be a successful math test taker, you need to read, think, and organize.

Read

Read each problem slowly and carefully. Look for words you don't know. Look at how those words fit in with the rest of the problem. Guess what they might mean.

Pretend you need to explain the problem to someone. Retell the problem in your own words.

Think

Decide what the problem is asking.

Most problems ask you to work with numbers.

EXAMPLE

It rained 8 days in May. It rained 7 days in June. It rained 4 days in July and 5 days in August. How many days did it rain during the summer?

You put all the days together. You have to **add**.
$8 + 7 + 4 + 5 = 24$ days

Some problems ask you to think about definitions of math terms (words).

EXAMPLE

Which triangles are **similar**?

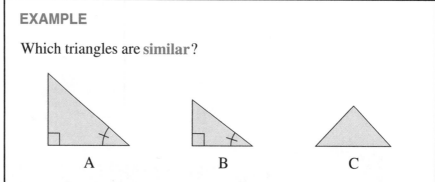

Definition: Similar triangles have equal angles.
Answer: Triangles A and B

Some problems ask you to use formulas.

EXAMPLE

What is the area of this rectangle?

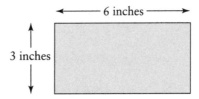

Use the **formula**: Area = length × width ($A = lw$)

6 inches × 3 inches = 18 square inches

Organize

If you can't understand the problem right away, stay calm and organize.

Ask yourself: "What do I need to know to find the right answer?"

Try to remember a problem you did before that looks like this problem.

Make a list of what you know and what you need to know.

EXAMPLE

Sherry takes three tests. She gets 89 on the first test, 85 on the second test, and 96 on the third test. What is her average score?

I know	I need to know
Scores on tests: 89 85 96	The average score

I need to do

Add the scores. Divide by 3.   ANSWER: The average score is 90.

You will learn useful strategies in every chapter. Use these successful strategies as you study and practice each lesson.

- Read the directions carefully. Ask the test-giver questions about the directions if you don't understand them.

- Answer the easy questions first.

- Estimate your answer.

- Ask yourself, *"Does this answer makes sense?"*

- Don't spend a lot of time on one question. Skip over it if you're stuck. You can look at it again after you answer the easy questions. Make sure you have enough time for all questions.

- Don't change an answer unless you are *sure* your first choice is wrong.

- Fill in the answer sheet carefully. Make sure you put your answer in the right place.

Chapter 2

Whole Numbers and Number Sense

Addition and Subtraction

Addition makes numbers *bigger*.
Subtraction makes numbers *smaller*.

EXAMPLE A

My name is ⎯J⎯i⎯m.   3 letters

My name is J⎯⎯⎯.   −2 letters (subtract 2 letters)

My name is Jim ⎯S⎯m⎯i⎯t⎯h.   +5 letters (add 5 letters)

EXAMPLE B

A Collection of Cats

LeeAnn has a cat.	1
Her friend gives her another cat.	$1 + 1 = 2$
The 2 cats have 5 kittens.	$2 + 5 = 7$
LeeAnn can't keep 7 cats. She sells 3 cats.	$7 - 3 = 4$
A neighbor takes 2 cats to his farm.	$4 - 2 = 2$
The father cat runs away.	$2 - 1 = 1$
LeeAnn has 1 cat.	1

EXAMPLE C

Sam has **$25**. He pays **$10** for a movie. Now he has **$15**. $25 - 10 = 15$

His dad gives him **$10**. Now he has **$25** again. $15 + 10 = 25$

Keys to Understanding

Signal Words: Addition

Words	Example	Equation
sum or **total**	What is the **sum** of 14 and 32? What is the **total** of 14 and 32?	$14 + 32 = 46$
altogether	Ashley has a bike. Sam has 2 bikes. How many bikes do they have **altogether**?	$1 + 2 = 3$
more	Sara sees 3 stars. Then she sees 3 **more**. How many stars does she see?	$3 + 3 = 6$
plus	Abel has 4 books in his locker **plus** 4 more in his backpack. How many books does he have?	$4 + 4 = 8$

Signal Words: Subtraction

Words	Example	Equation
minus	The box has 24 cookies **minus** 2 cookies I ate.	$24 - 2 = 22$
How much is left? **many are**	He has 8 slices of pizza. He eats 3 slices. **How many are left?**	$8 - 3 = 5$
difference	What is the **difference** between 46 and 35?	$46 - 35 = 11$
less than	12 is how much **less than** 29?	$29 - 12 = 17$

Strategies for Test-Taking Success: Math © Thomson Heinle. Photocopying this page is prohibited by law.

Keys to Understanding

Keys to Addition

To add 0:
Write the number. 0 is nothing. $8 + 0 = 8$ $0 + 5 = 5$

To add 1:
Write the **next** number. $1 + 5 = 6$ $7 + 1 = 8$

To add 10:
Write **1** and the number. $6 + 10 = 16$ $10 + 8 = 18$

Practice A: Add.

a. 10   **b.** 5   **c.** 14   **d.** 11   **e.** 10
   $\underline{+5}$ $\underline{+1}$ $\underline{+0}$ $\underline{+1}$ $\underline{+2}$

Keys to Understanding

Keys to Subtraction

To subtract 0:
Write the number again. 0 is nothing. $8 - 0 = 8$ $5 - 0 = 5$

To subtract 1:
Write the number just before. $3 - 1 = 2$ $7 - 1 = 6$

Practice B: Subtract.

a. 1   **b.** 7   **c.** 5   **d.** 9   **e.** 3   **f.** 4
   $\underline{-0}$ $\underline{-1}$ $\underline{-1}$ $\underline{-0}$ $\underline{-1}$ $\underline{-0}$

SEE PAGE 195 FOR ANSWERS.

Word Problems: Decide if you add or subtract. Write an equation.

EXAMPLE

Tom gives his girlfriend one rose. Then he gives her 12 more roses. How many roses does he give her altogether?

EQUATION: $\underline{1 + 12 = 13}$

Practice Problems

1. Souvong has 18 pieces of candy. He gives 7 to his sister, Lara. How much candy does he have left?

   EQUATION: _____

2. Julie buys two CDs. One CD has 12 songs, and the other CD has 14 songs. What is the total number of songs on the CDs?

   EQUATION: _____

Number Patterns: Write the next number.

EXAMPLE

| 0 | 1 | 1 | 2 | 3 | 5 | 8 | 13 | $\overset{?}{\underline{}}$ |

Pattern: Add the last two numbers to get the next number.

$$0 + 1 = \boxed{1} + 2 = \boxed{3} + 5 = \boxed{8} + 13 = \underline{21}$$

Practice: Write the next two numbers.

5   6   10   11   15   16   20   ___   ___

SEE PAGE 195 FOR ANSWERS.

Number Facts Table: Addition and Subtraction

NUMBER FACTS TABLE FOR ADDITION AND SUBTRACTION

+/−	0	1	2	③	4	5	6	7	8	9	10
1	1	2	3	4	5	6	7	8	9	10	11
②	2	3	4	5						11	12
3	3	4	5	6	7					12	13
4	4	5		7	8	9				13	14
5	5	6			9	10	11			14	15
6	6	7				11	12	13		15	16
7	7	8					13	14	15	16	17
8	8	9						15	16	17	18
9	9	10	11	12	13	14	15	16	17	18	19
10	10	11	12	13	14	15	16	17	18	19	20

TIP

Find the 3 in the left column. Find the 2 in the top row. They meet at 5, too.

To Add: Use the Number Facts Table for Addition and Subtraction.

$2 + 3 = 5$ and $3 + 2 = 5$

For $2 + 3$:

1. Find the 2 in the left column.
2. Find the 3 in the top row.
3. Go across the columns and down the rows.

The numbers meet, or intersect, at 5. So $2 + 3 = 5$.

Use the Number Facts Table. Add 9 + 6 and 6 + 9. Check the correct answer.

___ A. $9 + 6 = 12$ and $6 + 9 = 12$

___ B. $9 + 6 = 15$ and $6 + 9 = 15$

B is correct. Numbers 6 and 9 intersect (meet) at 15.

Fill in the Number Facts Table for Addition and Subtraction. Check your work on page 195.

To Subtract: Use the Number Facts Table for Addition and Subtraction.

For $5 - 2$ and $5 - 3$:

1. Start at **5** in the gray. Move to the blue.

2. Find the **3** in the top row.

3. Find the **2** in the left column.

4. So $5 - 3 = 2$ and $5 - 3 = 2$.

Use the table. Check the true statement.

— A. $11 - 5 = 6$

— B. $5 - 11 = 6$

A is true. Start in the gray to subtract. Then move to the blue.

Practice: Add or subtract. Write the correct answer.

a. 1	**b.** 3	**c.** 5	**d.** 7	**e.** 4	**f.** 6
+2	+4	+4	+ 6	+5	+7

g. 16	**h.** 12	**i.** 15	**j.** 11	**k.** 19	**l.** 14
−9	−6	−8	−6	−10	−5

SEE PAGE 195 FOR ANSWERS.

Strategy 4 — Understand Place Value

Ways to Count Pennies

Count 1 by 1.

Count 2 by 2.

Count by 10s.

Counting Money and Numbers

Money: Group by tens.

10 pennies = 1 dime

10 dimes = 1 dollar

To get more pennies, change the dime into pennies. To get more dimes, change the dollar into dimes.

Numbers: Group by tens.

10 ones = 10

10 tens = 100

To get more ones, change tens into ones. To get more hundreds, change hundreds into tens.

Hundreds Place	Tens Place	Ones Place	
Dollars	Dimes	Pennies	Amount
1	5	3	$1.53
2	2	7	$2.27
8	5	4	$8.54

Make Change: Change the bills into dimes and pennies.

You can change pennies to dimes. You can change dimes to pennies.

EXAMPLE A

bill = dimes

Karina needs 60¢ for a soft drink. She has a dollar. She asks Julie for change for the vending machine. Julie gives her 10 dimes. Now she can buy her drink.

$1.00 = 10 dimes   60¢ = 6 dimes

EXAMPLE B

bill = dimes   pennies

A bus ticket costs $1.55. Dan has a ten-dollar bill. His brother gives him 9 one-dollar bills, 9 dimes, and 10 pennies. Now he can buy his bus ticket.

$10 bill = 9 dollars + 9 dimes + 10 pennies

$1.55 = 1 dollar + 5 dimes + 5 pennies

Practice: Make change. Complete the table.

Have	Need	Change the Dollar	Pay
$1	65¢	9 dimes, 10 pennies	6 dimes, 5 pennies
$1	72¢		
$10	$3.40		
$10	$2.74		

SEE PAGE 195 FOR ANSWERS.

Write Numbers

111 = ONE HUNDRED ELEVEN		
1 Hundred	**1 Ten**	**1 One**
&&&&&&&&&& &&&&&&&&&& &&&&&&&&&& &&&&&&&&&& &&&&&&&&&& &&&&&&&&&& &&&&&&&&&& &&&&&&&&&& &&&&&&&&&& &&&&&&&&&&	&&&&&&&&&&	&

You can show numbers in many ways. You can change a hundred into tens. You can change a ten into ones.

Hundreds Place	+	Tens Place	+	Ones Place	=	Number
2 hundreds	+	4 tens	+	7 ones	=	
1 hundred	+	14 tens	+	7 ones	=	**247**
1 hundred	+	13 tens	+	17 ones	=	

Practice: Write the numbers in different ways.

__7__ hundreds	+	__3__ tens	+	__8__ ones	=	_738_
_____ hundreds	+	_____ tens	+	_____ ones	=	**738**
_____ hundreds	+	_____ tens	+	_____ ones	=	
_____ hundreds	+	_____ tens	+	_____ ones	=	
_____ hundreds	+	_____ tens	+	_____ ones	=	**325**
_____ hundreds	+	_____ tens	+	_____ ones	=	
_____ hundreds	+	_____ tens	+	_____ ones	=	
_____ hundreds	+	_____ tens	+	_____ ones	=	**629**
_____ hundreds	+	_____ tens	+	_____ ones	=	

SEE PAGE 196 FOR ANSWERS.

Add Large Numbers: Look, Think, Estimate

EXAMPLE A   **64 + 23 =**

Look	Think	Estimate
64 + 23 =	64 is about 60. 23 is about 20.	60 + 20 = 80 The answer is about 80.
Add the ones.	64 +23 ───── 7	ESTIMATE: The answer is about 80. ANSWER: 87
Add the tens.	64 +23 ───── 87	The estimate is close.

EXAMPLE B   **437 + 195 =**

Look	Think	Estimate
437 +195	437 is about 400. 195 is about 200.	400 + 200 = 600 The answer is about 600.

Add the ones. Put the ten in the tens place. Put the 2 in the ones place.	7 + 5 = 12 12 = 10 + 2	437 +195 ───── 12 437 +195 ───── 2
Add the tens. Put the hundred in the hundreds place. Put the 3 tens in the tens place.	10 + 30 + 90 = 130 130 = 100 + 30	1 437 +195 ───── 132 11 437 +195 ───── 32
Add the hundreds.	100 + 400 +100 = 600	11 437 The answer is 632. +195 The estimate is close. ───── 632

Subtract Large Numbers: Look, Think, Estimate

EXAMPLE A   67 − 32 =

Look	Think	Estimate
67 − 32 =	67 is about 70. 32 is about 30.	$70 - 30 = 40$ The answer is about 40.
Subtract the ones.	$\begin{array}{r} 67 \\ -32 \\ \hline 5 \end{array}$	ESTIMATE: The answer is about 40.
Subtract the tens.	$\begin{array}{r} 67 \\ -32 \\ \hline 35 \end{array}$	ANSWER: 35 The estimate is close.

EXAMPLE B   314 − 126 =

Look	Think	Estimate
$\begin{array}{r} 314 \\ -126 \\ \hline \end{array}$	314 is about 300. 126 is about 100.	$300 - 100 = 200$ The answer is about 200.

Subtract.

4 is smaller than 6. You cannot subtract 6 from 4. Take a ten from the tens place. Add it to the ones. Then subtract the ones.	$\begin{array}{r} 3\,1\,4 \\ -1\,2\,6 \\ \hline \end{array}$	$\begin{array}{r} 3\;0\;14 \\ -1\,2\;\;6 \\ \hline 8 \end{array}$
There are no tens. You cannot subtract. Break the hundreds into 2 hundreds and 10 tens. 300 = 200 + 10 tens Subtract the tens.	$\begin{array}{r} 3\;0\;14 \\ -1\,2\;\;6 \\ \hline 8 \end{array}$	$\begin{array}{r} 2\;10\;14 \\ -\,1\;\,2\;\,6 \\ \hline 8\;\;8 \end{array}$
Subtract the hundreds.	$\begin{array}{r} 2\;10\;14 \\ -1\;2\;\;6 \\ \hline 1\;8\;\;8 \end{array}$ The answer is 188. The estimate is close.	

Strategies for Test-Taking Success: Math © Thomson Heinle.
Photocopying this page is prohibited by law.

Word Problems: Do you add or subtract? Write an estimate. Write the equation.

EXAMPLE

Our flight is 1 hour and 35 minutes late. (60 minutes + 35 minutes = 95 minutes) Then we wait 45 minutes more. How long do we wait altogether?

First, we need to round the time.

Rounding:

95 minutes → 100 minutes

45 minutes → 50 minutes

ESTIMATE: $100 + 50 = 150$ about 150 minutes

EQUATION: $95 + 45 = 140$ minutes

Practice Problems

TIP

Use rounding to estimate.

If the number is 4 or smaller, round down.
44 → 40

If the number is 5 or larger, round up.
46 → 50

1. The flight from El Paso is due at 2:03. It arrives at 2:21. How many minutes late is it?

   ESTIMATE: _____

   EQUATION: _____

2. How many minutes late is the flight from San Diego?

   ESTIMATE: _____

   EQUATION: _____

3. Juan waits for the flight from Yuma. He is at the airport at 3:10. How long does he wait?

   ESTIMATE: _____

   EQUATION: _____

SEE PAGE 196 FOR ANSWERS.

Add and Subtract Very Large Numbers

Each number is ten times bigger than the number after it.

10,000s	1,000s	100s	10s	1s
ten thousands	thousands	hundreds	tens	ones
10 × thousands	10 × hundreds	10 × tens	10 × 1	

To add: Put hundreds with the hundreds. Put tens with the tens.

To subtract: Change the hundreds to tens. Change the tens to ones.

Example 1
```
 1 1
 3884
+ 645
─────
 4529
```

Example 2
```
  1
 3561
+9603
─────
13164
```

Example 3
```
 2093      1 10 9 3
- 562    -   5 6 2
         ──────────
           1 5 3 1
```

Example 4
```
 24572    2   3  14  16  12
- 2899   -0  -2  -8  -9  -9
         ──────────────────
          2   1   6   7   3
```

Word Problem: What do you subtract?

EXAMPLE

The Eiffel Tower in France is 984 feet tall. The Petronas Tower 1 in Malaysia is 1,483 feet tall. It is the tallest building in the world. What is the difference?

ESTIMATE: $1,500 - 1,000 = 500$ The difference is about 500 feet.

EQUATION: $1483 - 984 = 499$ The difference is 499 feet.

Practice Problem: Dieter takes a trip around the world. He goes from Dallas to Paris to Beijing and back to Dallas. How many miles does he fly?

Dallas to Paris	4,939 miles
Paris to Beijing	4,119 miles
Beijing to Dallas	6,999 miles

ESTIMATE: _____

EQUATION: _____

SEE PAGE 196 FOR ANSWERS.

Multiplication and Division

Multiplication is addition of the same groups.

★★★   ★★★   ★★★   ★★★   ★★★

Multiply 3 stars by 5 groups. $3 \times 5 = 15$

Division is separation of groups.

★★★/★★★/★★★/★★★/★★★

Divide 15 stars into 5 groups. $15 \div 5 = 3$

EXAMPLE A

A Party Story

Sam and Betty are together.	2 = Sam and Betty
They have 5 daughters.	5 + 2 = the family
Each daughter has a husband.	$5 \times 2 = 10$ = daughters and husbands
Sam and Betty have a party. the All the daughters and all the husbands are at Sam and Betty's party.	$6 \times 2 = 12$ There are twelve people at party.
All couples dance in pairs.	$12 \div 2 = 6$ There are six couples.
The daughters and their husbands go home.	$12 - 10 = 2$
Sam and Betty are together again.	2 = Sam and Betty

EXAMPLE B

Zahra packs 18 glasses in a box. She puts them in 3 rows with 6 glasses in each row.	$18 \div 3 = 6$
She unpacks the glasses in her new house. She unpacks 3 rows at a time. Each row has 6 glasses. She puts all eighteen together on the table.	$3 \times 6 = 18$

Keys to Understanding

Signal Words: Multiplication

product	What is the **product** of 6 × 4?	6 × 4 = 24
times	What is 8 **times** 5?	8 × 5 = 40
twice as many	One ticket costs $10. How much do **twice as many** tickets cost?	2 × $10 = $20

Signal Words: Division

divided by	How much is 15 **divided by** 3?	15 ÷ 3 = 5
each	Four candy bars cost $1. How much does **each** candy bar cost?	$1 ÷ 4 = 25¢
per	The cost is $20 for 10 people. What is the cost **per** person?	$20 ÷ 10 = $2
evenly	How much is $35 divided **evenly** among 7 people?	$35 ÷ 7 = $5

 # Keys to Understanding

Keys to Multiplication

Multiply by 0:
Zero is nothing. Any number times **0** is **0**. 3 × 0 = 0   98 × 0 = 0

Multiply by 1:
A number times **1** is the same number.   8 × 1 = 8   67 × 1 = 67

Multiply by 5:
The answer always has a **0** or a **5** in the ones place.   5 × 6 = 30   7 × 5 = 35

Multiply by 10:
A number times **10** has a **0** at the end.   2 × 10 = 20   18 × 10 = 180

Practice:

a. 3 × 0 =

b. 8 × 5 =

c. 6 × 5 =

d. 18 × 1 =

e. 1 × 12 =

f. 0 × 9 =

SEE PAGE 196 FOR ANSWERS.

NUMBER FACTS TABLE FOR MULTIPLICATION AND DIVISION

×/÷	0	1	2	3	4	5	6	7	8	9	10
1	0	1	2	3	4	5	6	7	8	9	10
2	0	2	4	6	8	10	12	14	16	18	20
3		3	6			15				27	30
4		4	8			20				36	40
5	0	5	10	15	20	25	30	35	40	45	50
6		6	12			30				54	60
7		7	14			35				63	70
8		8	16			40				72	80
9	0	9	18	27	36	45	54	63	72	81	90
10	0	10	20	30	40	50	60	70	80	90	100

TIP

Find the 3 in the left column. Find the 2 in the top row. They meet at ⑥. So $2 \times 3 = 6$ and $3 \times 2 = 6$.

To Multiply: Use the Number Facts Table for Multiplication and Division.

For 2×3:

1. Find the 2 in the left column.

2. Find the 3 in the top row.

3. Go across the columns and down the rows.

They meet, or intersect, at 6. So $2 \times 3 = 6$.

Fill in the Number Facts Table for Multiplication and Division. Check your work on page 196.

To Divide: Use the Number Facts Table for Multiplication and Division. Division is the opposite of multiplication.

For $6 \div 3$:

1. Look at the 6 again.

2. Look across the row to the left column. It is 2.

3. So $6 \div 3 = 2$ and $6 \div 2 = 3$.

Word Problems: Do you multiply or divide? Write an equation. Solve the problem.

Swimmer	Swimming Speed (miles per hour)
person	5
turtle	5
bear	6
whale	9

EXAMPLE

A girl swims for 5 hours. How far does she swim?

EQUATION: $5 \times 5 = 25$ miles

Practice Problems

1. A bear swims for 4 hours. How far does it go?

   EQUATION: _____

2. A boy and a bear race to an island. They swim 30 miles. How much sooner does the bear get to the island?

   EQUATION: _____

3. A turtle swims for 5 hours. A whale swims for 3 hours. Which animal swims more miles?

   EQUATION: _____

Order of Operations

Sometimes you add, subtract, multiply, and/or divide in one equation.

There are rules about what to do first, second, and third.

1. Do what is in *parentheses* ( ) first.	$3 \times (4 + 2) - 8 =$ _____ $3 \times 6 - 8 =$ _____
2. Next, multiply or divide.	$3 \times 6 - 8 =$ _____ $18 - 8 =$
3. Last, add or subtract.	$18 - 8 = 10$

Practice:

a. $(3 \times 7) - 3 =$ **b.** $4 \times 6 - 10 =$ **c.** $(2 + 10) + (3 \times 5) =$

SEE PAGE 197 FOR ANSWERS.

Strategy 7 Multiply Large Numbers

Step 1

Multiply the ones.	1
Put the tens with the tens.	433
	× 5
	5

Think: $5 \times 3 = 15$
$15 = 5$ ones and 1 ten
Put the 5 ones in the ones place.
Put the 10 in the tens place.

Step 2

Multiply the tens.	11
Add the extra ten.	433
Put the hundred with the	× 5
hundreds.	65

Think: 5×3 tens = 15 tens
15 tens + 1 ten = 16 tens
16 tens = 10 tens + 6 tens
10 tens = 100
Put the 6 tens in the tens place.
Put the hundred with the hundreds.

Step 3

Multiply the hundreds.	11
Add the extra hundred.	433
	× 5
	2165

Think: 5×4 hundreds = 20 hundreds
20 hundreds + 1 hundred = 21 hundreds
21 hundreds = 2 thousands and 1 hundred

Practice: Multiply. Write the correct answers.

a. 426 × 2   b. 358 × 3   c. 591 × 6   d. 228 × 7   e. 392 × 8

SEE PAGE 197 FOR ANSWERS.

Keys to Understanding

More Keys to Multiplication

To multiply a number by 10:
Put 0 after the number.

$10 \times 3 = 30$ $10 \times 15 = 150$

To multiply by 100:
Put 00 after the number.

$100 \times 32 = 3200$ $100 \times 415 = 41500$

To multiply by 1000:
Put 000 after the number.

$1000 \times 32 = 32000$ $1000 \times 415 = 415000$

Practice A: Multiply. Write the correct answer.

a. 8   **b.** 66   **c.** 29   **d.** 795   **e.** 483   **f.** 567
    ×10   ×1000   ×100   ×1000   ×10   ×100

Practice B: Complete the table.

EXAMPLE

There are 100 pennies in a dollar. How many pennies are in 3 dollars? How many dimes are in 3 dollars?

$100 \times 3 = 300$ $10 \times 3 = 30$

How many pennies?	How many dimes?
$3 = 300 pennies	$3 = 30 dimes
$5 =	$5 =
$13 =	$13 =
$21 =	$21 =

SEE PAGE 197 FOR ANSWERS.

Multiply by Two Numbers

EXAMPLE A

Step 1

Multiply by the ones.

$$\begin{array}{r} 15 \\ \times\ 12 \\ \hline 30 \end{array}$$

Think: $2 \times 15 = 30$

Step 2

Multiply by the tens.

$$\begin{array}{r} 15 \\ \times\ 12 \\ \hline 30 \\ 150 \end{array}$$

Think: $10 \times 15 = 150$

Step 3

Add the two answers together.

$$\begin{array}{r} 15 \\ \times\ 12 \\ \hline 30 \\ +150 \\ \hline 180 \end{array}$$

Think: $30 + 150 = 180$

EXAMPLE B

Step 1

Multiply by the ones.

$$\begin{array}{r} 104 \\ \times\ 21 \\ \hline 104 \end{array}$$

Think: $1 \times 104 = 104$

Step 2

Multiply by the tens.

$$\begin{array}{r} 104 \\ \times\ 21 \\ \hline 104 \\ 2080 \end{array}$$

Think: $2 \times 104 = 208$
$10 \times 208 = 2080$

Step 3

Add the two answers together.

$$\begin{array}{r} 104 \\ \times\ 21 \\ \hline 104 \\ +2080 \\ \hline 2184 \end{array}$$

Think: $104 + 2080 = 2184$

Multiply by Three Numbers

EXAMPLE

Step 1

Multiply by the ones.

```
   230
 ×105
  1150
```

Think: $5 \times 230 = 1150$

Step 2

Multiply by the tens.

```
   230
 ×105
  1150
     0
```

Think: $0 \times 230 = 0$

Step 3

Multiply by the hundreds.

```
    230
  ×105
   1150
      0
  23000
```

Think: $100 \times 230 = 23000$

Step 4

Add the three answers together.

```
    230
  ×105
   1150
      0
 +23000
  24150
```

Think: $1150 + 0 + 23000 = 24150$

Word Problems: Estimate and multiply. Write an estimate and an equation. Solve the problem.

EXAMPLE

There are 28 deer in a square mile. How many deer are in 12 square miles?

ESTIMATE: 28 is about 30. 12 is about 10. $30 \times 10 = 300$

EQUATION: $28 \times 12 = 336$ There are 336 deer in 12 square miles.

Practice Problems:

1. Ali buys 19 CDs. She pays $17 for each CD. How much does she spend?

   ESTIMATE: _____

   EQUATION: _____

2. There are 23 flights between New York and Chicago every day. January has 31 days. How many flights are there in January?

   ESTIMATE: _____

   EQUATION: _____

3. Kim baby-sits for 63 days. She makes $26 a day. How much money does she make?

   ESTIMATE: _____

   EQUATION: _____

4. A store buys 106 boxes of pens. Every box has 144 pens. What is the total number of pens in the store?

   ESTIMATE: _____

   EQUATION: _____

SEE PAGE 197 FOR ANSWERS.

Divide Larger Numbers

This is how you divide a very big number. Divide the biggest number first.

Divide the hundreds. Then, divide the tens. Last, divide the ones.

EXAMPLE A

Step 1

Write the problem like this: $2\overline{)842}$

Step 2

Divide the hundreds.

$$
\begin{array}{r}
400 \\
2\overline{)842} \\
800
\end{array}
$$

Think: $2 \times 400 = 800$

Step 3

Subtract.

$$
\begin{array}{r}
400 \\
2\overline{)842} \\
- 800 \\
\hline
42
\end{array}
$$

Think: $842 - 800 = 42$

Step 4

Divide the tens.

$$
\begin{array}{r}
20 \\
400 \\
2\overline{)842} \\
800 \\
\hline
42 \\
40
\end{array}
$$

Think: $2 \times 20 = 40$

Step 5

Subtract.
Divide the ones.

$$
\begin{array}{r}
1 \\
20 \\
400 \\
2\overline{)842} \\
800 \\
\hline
42 \\
- 40 \\
\hline
2 \\
2
\end{array}
$$

Think: $42 - 40 = 2$
Think: $2 \times 1 = 2$

Step 6

Add all the answers.

$$
\begin{array}{r}
1 \\
20 \\
400 \\
2\overline{)842} \\
800 \\
\hline
42 \\
- 40 \\
\hline
2 \\
- 2 \\
\hline
0
\end{array}
$$

The answer is 421.

Think: $400 + 20 + 1 = 421$

EXAMPLE B

Step 1

Write the problem
like this: 3)609

Step 2

Divide the hundreds.

$$
\begin{array}{r}
200 \\
3\overline{)609} \\
600 \\
\hline
\end{array}
$$

Step 3

Subtract.

$$
\begin{array}{r}
200 \\
3\overline{)609} \\
-\ 600 \\
\hline
9
\end{array}
$$

Step 4

Divide the tens.
If there are no tens, put a
zero in the tens' place.

$$
\begin{array}{r}
00 \\
200 \\
3\overline{)609} \\
600 \\
\hline
9
\end{array}
$$

Step 5

Divide the ones.
Subtract.

$$
\begin{array}{r}
3 \\
00 \\
200 \\
3\overline{)609} \\
600 \\
\hline
9 \\
-\ 9 \\
\hline
0
\end{array}
$$

Step 6

Add all the answers.

$$
\begin{array}{r}
3 \\
00 \\
200 \\
3\overline{)609} \\
600 \\
\hline
9 \\
-\ 9 \\
\hline
0
\end{array}
$$

The answer is 203.

You can do a division problem without the zeros, too.

Step 1

$$
\begin{array}{r}
2 \\
3\overline{)609} \\
600 \\
\hline
\end{array}
$$

Step 2

$$
\begin{array}{r}
20 \\
3\overline{)609} \\
600 \\
\hline
\end{array}
$$

Step 3

$$
\begin{array}{r}
203 \\
3\overline{)609} \\
600 \\
\hline
9 \\
-\ 9 \\
\hline
0
\end{array}
$$

Practice: Estimate and divide.

a. 2)448   **b.** 16)160   **c.** 5)100
d. 32)608   **e.** 21)630

SEE PAGE 197 FOR ANSWERS.

Word Problem: Some butterflies fly 4,000 miles to their winter home. Some butterflies fly 5 mph (miles per hour). Others fly 25 mph. Most butterflies live about a week. Some butterflies live 9 months.

EXAMPLE

One butterfly lives 360 hours. How many days does it live?

(24 hours = 1 day)

ESTIMATE: $400 \div 20 = 20$ 360 hours is about 20 days.

EQUATION: $360 \div 24 = 15$ days. The butterfly lives 15 days.

Practice Problems

1. A butterfly flies 3,990 miles. The trip takes 42 days. How many miles does it fly in a day?

   ESTIMATE: _____

   EQUATION: _____

2. A butterfly flies 25 mph for 1,250 miles. How many hours does the butterfly take to fly home?

   ESTIMATE: _____

   EQUATION: _____

3. A butterfly flies 55 miles per day. How many days does it take to fly 1,815 miles?

   ESTIMATE: _____

   EQUATION: _____

SEE PAGE 197 FOR ANSWERS.

Now use your whole number skills to take a Review Test.

CHAPTER 2: REVIEW TEST

Mark your answers on the Answer Grid.

1 It snows 11 inches on Monday plus another 7 inches on Tuesday. How much does it snow on both days?

   A 4

   B 18

   C 77

   D 89

2 Carl had 6 pieces of gum in his pocket. 4 pieces of gum fall out. How many pieces does he have now?

   A 0

   B 2

   C 6

   D 10

3 Amelia takes 45 minutes to clean her room. She takes 30 minutes to do the dishes. How many minutes does she take to do both jobs?

   A 15 minutes

   B 45 minutes

   C 70 minutes

   D 75 minutes

4 Alex makes 45 cookies for his class at school minus 6 cookies for his brother. How many cookies does he bring to school?

   A 31

   B 39

   C 45

   D 51

5 A basketball team scores 46 points in the first half of a game. The team scores 64 points in the second half. What is the total number of points they score?

   A 20

   B 64

   C 100

   D 110

6 A race car goes 115 mph (miles per hour). It slows down to 48 mph at corners. What is the difference between the two speeds?

   A 3 mph

   B 67 mph

   C 73 mph

   D 133 mph

GO ON

7 Hassim has to write a 250-word paper. He writes 127 words. How many more words does he have to write?

A   23 words

B   123 words

C   137 words

D   377 words

8 Sheila talks on the telephone 15 minutes a day. How many minutes does she talk in a week?

A   15 minutes

B   20 minutes

C   73 minutes

D   105 minutes

9 Three boys take turns waiting to buy tickets. Each boy waits the same number of minutes. They wait 45 minutes altogether. How long does each boy wait?

A   15

B   30

C   42

D   45

10 Ali makes $6 per hour. He works 8 hours a day. How much does he make in a day?

A $12

B $14

C $16

D $48

11 Nina takes medicine every 4 hours. There are 24 hours in a day. How many times per day does she take medicine?

A   4 times

B   6 times

C   16 times

D   20 times

12 Marisa puts 12 donuts in a box at the donut shop. She has 13 boxes. How many donuts does she need?

A   12

B   25

C   105

D   156

GO ON

13 Mr. Lee and his family drive 1,260 miles on their vacation. They drive 420 miles each day. How many days do they drive?

A 2 days

B 3 days

C 33 days

D 840 days

14 Johann wants to buy a bicycle for $440. He makes $11 an hour. How many hours does he have to work to make $440?

A 40 hours

B 44 hours

C 451 hours

D 4,840 hours

15 Luis has $65 to spend. He spends a little each day. Look at the pattern in the table. How much money does he have left on Friday?

Day	Amount
Sunday	$65
Monday	$55
Tuesday	$50
Wednesday	$40
Thursday	$35
Friday	

A $15

B $20

C $25

D $30

STOP. THIS IS THE END OF THE REVIEW TEST.
SEE PAGE 198 FOR ANSWERS AND EXPLANATIONS.

Chapter

3

Fractions, Decimals, and Percents

Strategies for Test-Taking Success: Math © Thomson Heinle.
Photocopying this page is prohibited by law.

Strategy 9

Describe Fractions

A fraction can be part of a group.

3/4's of teenagers prefer Goodlicks Ice Cream

or

A fraction can be part of a whole.

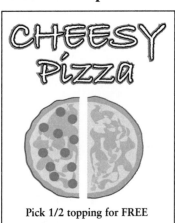

Pick 1/2 topping for FREE

Winning and Losing at Big City High School	
Big City High School has 5 teams.	5
Four of the teams win: the basketball team, the baseball team, the track team, and the tennis team.	$\frac{4}{5}$ = 4 out of 5 teams
One team loses: the football team.	$\frac{1}{5}$ = 1 out of 5 teams
Coach Kane says, "We have 18 football players. 9 players are freshmen. Wait until next year!"	$\frac{9}{18}$ = 9 out of 18 players

Fraction Names

TIP

The denominator is
down.

$\frac{2}{3}$ numerator
denominator

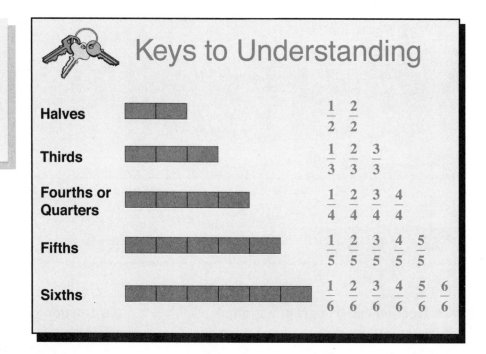

Keys to Understanding

Halves		$\frac{1}{2}$ $\frac{2}{2}$
Thirds		$\frac{1}{3}$ $\frac{2}{3}$ $\frac{3}{3}$
Fourths or Quarters		$\frac{1}{4}$ $\frac{2}{4}$ $\frac{3}{4}$ $\frac{4}{4}$
Fifths		$\frac{1}{5}$ $\frac{2}{5}$ $\frac{3}{5}$ $\frac{4}{5}$ $\frac{5}{5}$
Sixths		$\frac{1}{6}$ $\frac{2}{6}$ $\frac{3}{6}$ $\frac{4}{6}$ $\frac{5}{6}$ $\frac{6}{6}$

TIP

You can write
fractions
up and down: $\frac{1}{2}$

or across: 1/2

Read the fraction name. Write the correct fraction from the box.

$\frac{2}{3}$	$\frac{1}{2}$	$\frac{1}{4}$	$\frac{3}{4}$	$\frac{3}{5}$	$\frac{1}{6}$

EXAMPLE

(a quarter) $\frac{1}{4}$ of a dollar

a. (half) _____ of a pie

b. (two-thirds) _____ of the class

c. (one-sixth) _____ of a foot

d. (three-fourths) _____ of the candy

e. (three-fifths) _____ of the circle

ANSWERS: a. $\frac{1}{2}$ b. $\frac{2}{3}$ c. $\frac{1}{6}$ d. $\frac{3}{4}$ e. $\frac{3}{5}$

Fraction Pictures

TIP

Numerator = colored pieces only
Denominator = ALL pieces

One half is

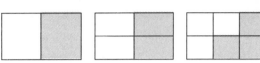

1 out of 2	2 out of 4	3 out of 6
$\dfrac{1}{2}$	$= \quad \dfrac{2}{4}$	$= \quad \dfrac{3}{6}$

One-third is

1 out of 3   2 out of 6

$$\frac{1}{3} \quad = \quad \frac{2}{6}$$

Two-thirds are

2 out of 3   4 out of 6

$$\frac{2}{3} \quad = \quad \frac{4}{6}$$

Practice A: Write the fraction name of the colored part. Use the fractions in the box.

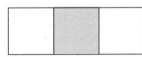

$$\frac{1}{2} \qquad \frac{1}{3} \qquad \frac{2}{6}$$

$\dfrac{1}{3}$ **a.** _____   **b.** _____

Practice B: Circle the bigger fraction.

$\boxed{\dfrac{1}{2}}$ or $\dfrac{1}{4}$ **a.** $\dfrac{1}{5}$ or $\dfrac{1}{4}$ **b.** $\dfrac{1}{6}$ or $\dfrac{2}{3}$ **c.** $\dfrac{2}{4}$ or $\dfrac{4}{6}$

SEE PAGE 199 FOR ANSWERS.

Add and Subtract Fractions with the Same Denominator

EXAMPLE A   **John and the Pizza**

John has a pizza. He cuts it into six pieces

He eats two pieces. He is still hungry.

He eats three more pieces. He is still hungry.

He eats one more piece. He is still hungry.

He orders another pizza. He cuts the pizza into six pieces.

$$\frac{6}{6}$$

$$\frac{6}{6} - \frac{2}{6} = \frac{4}{6}$$

$$\frac{4}{6} - \frac{3}{6} = \frac{1}{6}$$

$$\frac{1}{6} - \frac{1}{6} = 0$$

$$\frac{6}{6}$$

EXAMPLE B   **Big Enough to Ride**

44 INCHES TALL

Ashley wants to ride the Bumper Cars. She is 43 inches tall.

43 inches

She grows $\frac{2}{4}$ of an inch in June.

$43 + \frac{2}{4} = 43\frac{2}{4}$ inches

She grows $\frac{1}{4}$ inch in July.

$43\frac{2}{4} + \frac{1}{4} = 43\frac{3}{4}$ inches

She does not grow in August.

$43\frac{3}{4} + 0 = 43\frac{3}{4}$ inches

She grows $\frac{1}{4}$ inch in September.

$43\frac{3}{4} + \frac{1}{4} = 43 + \frac{4}{4}$ inches $= 43 + 1 = 44$ inches

Now, Ashley can ride those Bumper Cars!

TIP

To add or subtract fractions with the same denominator, add or subtract the numerators.

$$\frac{2}{4} + \frac{1}{4} = \frac{3}{4}$$

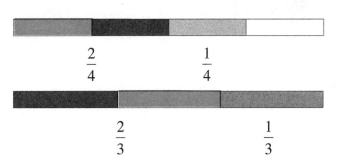

$$\frac{2}{3} - \frac{1}{3} = \frac{1}{3}$$

$\frac{2}{4}$ $\frac{1}{4}$

$\frac{2}{3}$ $\frac{1}{3}$

Practice:

EXAMPLE

$\frac{4}{5} - \frac{1}{5} = \frac{3}{5}$ **a.** $\frac{1}{3} + \frac{2}{3} =$ **b.** $\frac{5}{6} - \frac{3}{6} =$ **c.** $\frac{2}{5} + \frac{2}{5} =$

Word Problems: Do you add or subtract? Write an estimate and an equation. Solve the problem.

EXAMPLE

John went to see his girlfriend. He walked $\frac{1}{3}$ of a mile. Then he ran $\frac{1}{3}$ of a mile. How far did he go altogether?

ESTIMATE: $1 + 1 = 2$ EQUATION: $\frac{1}{3} + \frac{1}{3} = \frac{2}{3}$ of a mile

Practice Problems

1. Shurtika sells meat. She has $\frac{3}{4}$ of a pound of ham. She sells $\frac{1}{4}$ of a pound. How much ham is left?

   ESTIMATE: _____

   EQUATION: _____

2. Marina bakes two cakes. She puts $\frac{1}{4}$ cup of frosting on the small cake and $\frac{2}{4}$ cup of frosting on the large cake. How much frosting does she use altogether?

   ESTIMATE: _____

   EQUATION: _____

3. $\frac{4}{5}$ of the students buy balloons at the picnic. $\frac{1}{5}$ of the balloons break. Now how many students have balloons?

   ESTIMATE: _____

   EQUATION: _____

   SEE PAGE 199 FOR ANSWERS.

Multiply Fractions

Show Division with Fractions

There are three ways to divide 8 by 4: $8 \div 4 = 2$ $4\overline{)8}^{\,2}$ $\dfrac{8}{4} = 2$

Divide.

$\dfrac{6}{2} = 3$ **a.** $\dfrac{9}{3} =$ **b.** $\dfrac{4}{1} =$ **c.** $\dfrac{6}{3} =$ **d.** $\dfrac{8}{2} =$ **e.** $\dfrac{10}{5} =$

ANSWERS a. 3   b. 4   c. 2   d. 4   e. 2

Any number can be a fraction. You can write whole numbers as fractions.

$$\dfrac{\text{Numerator}}{\text{Denominator}} = \dfrac{\text{pieces you have}}{\text{all the pieces}}$$

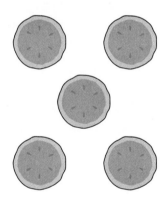

Here is one pie.

The pie is in 5 pieces.

$1 \div 5 = \dfrac{1}{5}$

Each piece is $\dfrac{1}{5}$ of the pie.

Here are 5 pies.

Each pie is 1 piece.

$1 \div 5 = \dfrac{1}{5}$

Each pie is $\dfrac{1}{5}$ of the pies.

 # Keys to Understanding

Division with Fractions

Dividing a number by 1, you get the same number.

$$\frac{4}{1} = 4 \qquad\qquad \frac{25}{1} = 25$$

Dividing a number by itself, you get 1.

$$\frac{4}{4} = 1 \qquad\qquad \frac{25}{25} = 1$$

Divide. Write the correct answer.

$$\frac{4}{1} = 4 \qquad \textbf{a.}\ \frac{7}{1} = \qquad \textbf{b.}\ \frac{8}{1} = \qquad \textbf{c.}\ \frac{4}{4} = \qquad \textbf{d.}\ \frac{7}{7} = \qquad \textbf{e.}\ \frac{8}{8} =$$

ANSWERS: a. 7   b. 8   c. 1   d. 1   e. 1

$$\frac{1}{2} \times \frac{10}{1} = \frac{10}{2} = \frac{5}{1}$$

The steps to multiply fractions are:

$$\frac{1}{2} \text{ of } 8 = \frac{1}{2} \times \frac{8}{1} = 4$$

Step A: Multiply the numerators.

$$\frac{1}{2} \times \frac{8}{1} = \frac{8}{}$$

Step B: Multiply the denominators.

$$\frac{1}{2} \times \frac{8}{1} = \frac{8}{2}$$

Step C: Divide the numerator by the denominator.

$$\frac{8}{2} = 4$$

Word Problems: Multiply fractions.

EXAMPLE

Carlos writes 6 letters. He mails half the letters. He mails 3 letters.

ESTIMATE: Half of 6 is 3.

EQUATION: $\dfrac{1}{2} \times \dfrac{6}{1} = \dfrac{6}{2} = 3$

Practice Problems

1. Max has 10 dimes. He spends $\frac{1}{2}$ of them. How many dimes does he spend?

    ESTIMATE: _____

    EQUATION: _____

2. Edith buys 9 soft drinks. She drinks $\frac{1}{3}$ of them. How many does she drink?

    ESTIMATE: _____

    EQUATION: _____

3. Stanley plays 8 songs on the piano. $\frac{1}{4}$ of the songs are new. How many are new?

    ESTIMATE: _____

    EQUATION: _____

SEE PAGE 199 FOR ANSWERS.

 Keys to Understanding

Equivalent means *equal*.

3 and **three** are **equivalent**.

3 or three = △ △ △

$6 \div 3$, $3\overline{)6}$, and $\dfrac{6}{3}$ are **equivalent**.

$6 \div 3$, $3\overline{)6}$, and $\dfrac{6}{3}$ = 6 divided by 3

$\dfrac{1}{2}$ and one-half are **equivalent**.

$\dfrac{1}{2}$ and one-half = $\bigcirc$

A fraction equals 1 when the numerator equals the denominator.

$$\frac{5}{5} = 1 \qquad \frac{3}{3} = 1 \qquad \frac{10}{10} = 1$$

Make an equivalent fraction	
Step A: Choose a fraction that equals one.	I choose $\frac{4}{4}$.
Step B: Multiply a fraction with the fraction that equals one.	$\frac{1}{2} \times \frac{4}{4} = \frac{4}{8}$
Step C: Get an equivalent fraction.	$\frac{4}{8} = \frac{1}{2} \quad \frac{4}{8}$ is equivalent to $\frac{1}{2}$.

Keys to Understanding

Multiplying by one changes a fraction's **name**.

$$\frac{1}{2} \times \frac{2}{2} = \frac{2}{4} \qquad \frac{1}{2} \times \frac{3}{3} = \frac{3}{6}$$

These are all equivalent fractions.
They all equal one-half.

Multiplying by one does **not** change a fraction's **value**.

$$\frac{1}{2} \times \frac{4}{4} = \frac{4}{8} \qquad \frac{1}{2} \times \frac{5}{5} = \frac{5}{10}$$

$$\frac{1}{2} = \frac{2}{4} = \frac{3}{6} = \frac{4}{8} = \frac{5}{10}$$

Circle the fractions that equal $\frac{1}{3}$.

$$\frac{3}{4} \qquad \frac{2}{6} \qquad \frac{3}{6} \qquad \frac{3}{9} \qquad \frac{4}{12}$$

ANSWERS: $\frac{1}{3} \times \frac{2}{2} = \frac{2}{6} \qquad \frac{1}{3} \times \frac{3}{3} = \frac{3}{9} \qquad \frac{1}{3} \times \frac{4}{4} = \frac{4}{12}$

Strategy 12	Add and Subtract Fractions with Different Denominators

EXAMPLE A

Charlie eats $\frac{1}{4}$ of a cherry pie. Then he eats $\frac{1}{2}$ of an apple pie.

How much pie does Charlie eat altogether?

Remember: You can't add $\frac{1}{4}$ and $\frac{1}{2}$ until they have the same denominator.

Step A: Write the problem. $\frac{1}{4} + \frac{1}{2}$ You must **change** the **half** to **fourths**.	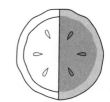
Step B: Multiply by one. $\frac{2}{2} \times \frac{1}{2} = \frac{2}{4}$	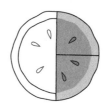
Step C: Write the problem again. $\frac{1}{4} + \frac{2}{4}$	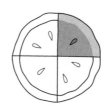 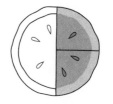
Step D: Add the numerators. $\frac{1}{4} + \frac{2}{4} = \frac{3}{4}$	Charlie eats $\frac{3}{4}$ of a pie altogether.

Strategies for Test-Taking Success:: Math © Thomson Heinle. Photocopying this page is prohibited by law.

58 Chapter 3 Fractions, Decimals, and Percents

EXAMPLE B

It snows $\frac{2}{3}$ of an inch. Then $\frac{1}{2}$ of an inch of snow melts.
How much snow is left?

Remember: You can't subtract $\frac{1}{2}$ from $\frac{2}{3}$. The denominators must be the same.

Step A: Write the problem. $\dfrac{2}{3} - \dfrac{1}{2}$ You must change both fractions to **sixths**.	$2 \times 3 = 6$ $3 \times 2 = 6$
Step B: Multiply both fractions by one to get 6 in the denominator. $\dfrac{2}{2} \times \dfrac{2}{3} = \dfrac{4}{6}$ $\qquad$ $\dfrac{3}{3} \times \dfrac{1}{2} = \dfrac{3}{6}$	$\dfrac{2}{2} = 1$ $\quad$ $\dfrac{3}{3} = 1$
Step C: Write the problem again. $\dfrac{4}{6} - \dfrac{3}{6}$	
Step D: Subtract the numerators. $\dfrac{4}{6} - \dfrac{3}{6} = \dfrac{1}{6}$	$\dfrac{1}{6}$ of an inch of snow is left.

Word Problems: Do you add or subtract? Solve the problem.

EXAMPLE

An inchworm crawls across a leaf. It crawls $\frac{1}{3}$ of an inch. Later it crawls $\frac{1}{2}$ an inch. How far does it crawl?

ESTIMATE: $\frac{1}{3}$ is less than $\frac{1}{2}$. $\qquad\qquad$ EQUATION: $\frac{1}{3} + \frac{1}{2}$

$\frac{1}{2} + \frac{1}{2} = \frac{2}{2} = 1$ $\qquad\qquad\qquad\qquad$ $\frac{2}{6} + \frac{3}{6} = \frac{5}{6}$ of an inch

$\frac{1}{3} + \frac{1}{2}$ is less than 1.

Practice Problems: Write an estimate and an equation.

1. José looks at his box of cereal. It was $\frac{3}{4}$ full yesterday morning. It is only $\frac{1}{2}$ full now. How much of the cereal did he eat?

2. Alex is 6 feet and $\frac{3}{4}$ of an inch. Tom is 6 feet and $\frac{1}{2}$ of an inch. How much taller is Alex?

3. Olga has a lot of homework tonight. She works $\frac{1}{4}$ of an hour on English, $\frac{1}{2}$ an hour on history, and $\frac{1}{4}$ of an hour on math. How long does Olga do homework?

SEE PAGE 199 FOR ANSWERS.

Divide and Simplify Fractions

Divide Fractions

How many **halves** are in 6? $6 \div \frac{1}{2} = 12$
There are **12** halves in **6**.

A Quick Trick to Divide Fractions: Turn the 2nd fraction over and multiply.

Step A: Write the problem. $\frac{4}{1} \div \frac{1}{3}$

How many **one-thirds** are in **4**?

| 1 | 2 | 3 | 4 |

$\frac{1}{3}$ $\frac{1}{3}$ $\frac{1}{3}$ $\frac{1}{3}$ $\frac{1}{3}$ $\frac{1}{3}$ $\frac{1}{3}$ $\frac{1}{3}$ $\frac{1}{3}$ $\frac{1}{3}$ $\frac{1}{3}$ $\frac{1}{3}$

Step B: Turn the 2nd fraction over.

$\frac{4}{1} \div \frac{3}{1}$

Step C: Multiply. $\frac{4}{1} \times \frac{3}{1} = \frac{12}{1}$

There are **12 one-thirds** in **4**.

Word Problems: Divide fractions.

EXAMPLE

A board is three feet long. George cuts the board into pieces. Each piece is one foot long. How many pieces does George have altogether?

ESTIMATE: There are about 6 halves in 3.   EQUATION: $\frac{3}{1} \div \frac{1}{2} = 6$

Practice Problems: Write an estimate and an equation.

1. It takes Kolby $\frac{1}{4}$ an hour to run around the track. He runs for 2 hours. How many times does he go around the track?

2. Sue is making a design on a poster. She is using $\frac{1}{4}$-inch strips of paper. She has a space that is $\frac{6}{8}$ of an inch wide. How many strips of paper can she use?

SEE PAGE 200 FOR ANSWERS.

Simplify Fractions

Key to Understanding

Find the simplest fraction.

Three words, one meaning: **simplify, reduce, convert**

Signal Directions: **Simplify** your answer.

Reduce the fractions.

Convert the fractions to their simplest forms.

1. Find the simplest equivalent fraction.		**2. Take out ones.**
$$\frac{4}{8} = \frac{3}{6} = \frac{2}{4} = \frac{1}{2}$$	or	$$\frac{3}{2} - \frac{2}{2} = \frac{1}{2}$$
$\left(\frac{1}{2}\right)$ is the simplest equivalent fraction.		

Two Ways to Simplify a Fraction

1. Divide the numerator and denominator by the same number:

$$\frac{3}{6} \qquad \begin{array}{l} 3 \div 3 = 1 \\ 6 \div 3 = 2 \end{array} \qquad \frac{3}{6} = \frac{1}{2}$$

$$\frac{6}{8} \qquad \begin{array}{l} 6 \div 2 = 3 \\ 8 \div 2 = 4 \end{array} \qquad \frac{6}{8} = \frac{3}{4}$$

2. Change to a whole number plus a fraction. These are **mixed numbers**.

A whole number plus a fraction = a fraction with a numerator bigger than the denominator.

$$\frac{5}{4} = 1\frac{1}{4} \qquad\qquad \frac{6}{3} = 2 \qquad\qquad \frac{5}{2} = 2\frac{1}{2}$$

Simplify the fraction. Change the fraction to a whole number plus a fraction.

Subtract ones. Write the ones plus the fraction.

$\frac{5}{4} - \frac{4}{4} = \frac{1}{4}$	$\frac{6}{3} - \frac{3}{3} - \frac{3}{3} = 0$	$\frac{5}{2} - \frac{2}{2} - \frac{2}{2} = \frac{1}{2}$
$\frac{4}{4} + \frac{1}{4} = 1\frac{1}{4}$	$\frac{3}{3} + \frac{3}{3} = 2$	$\frac{2}{2} + \frac{2}{2} + \frac{1}{2} = 2\frac{1}{2}$

Practice: Simplify the fractions.

$\frac{6}{8} = \frac{3}{4}$ **a.** $\frac{2}{4}$ **b.** $\frac{4}{6}$ **c.** $\frac{3}{2}$ **d.** $\frac{8}{3}$ **e.** $\frac{6}{4}$

Word Problems: Add or subtract. Convert the answers to the simplest form.

EXAMPLE

Cathy makes cookies. She measures $\frac{2}{3}$ of a cup of sugar. Then she adds another $\frac{2}{3}$ of a cup of sugar. How much sugar does she use?

ESTIMATE: $2 + 2 = 4 \frac{4}{3}$ is more than 1

EQUATION: $\frac{2}{3} + \frac{2}{3} = \frac{4}{3} = 1\frac{1}{3}$

Practice Problems

1. It snows $\frac{5}{6}$ of an inch on Sunday. $\frac{1}{6}$ of an inch of snow melts on Monday. How much snow is left?

   ESTIMATE: _____

   EQUATION: _____

2. Jorge borrows $\frac{3}{4}$ of a dollar from Sam, $\frac{1}{2}$ of a dollar from Bill, and $\frac{1}{4}$ of a dollar from Mary. How much money does he borrow?

   ESTIMATE: _____

   EQUATION: _____

SEE PAGE 200 FOR ANSWERS.

Compare Decimals and Fractions

Decimals and fractions show **parts of things**. You can write decimals as fractions.

Some decimals are fractions with **10** in their **denominators**.

EXAMPLE: $\frac{1}{10} = .1$

These decimals have **one place**. They are called **tenths**.

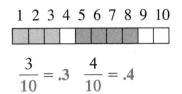

$$\frac{3}{10} = .3 \quad \frac{4}{10} = .4$$

Write these fractions as decimals.

$\frac{3}{10} = .3$ **a.** $\frac{8}{10}$ **b.** $\frac{1}{10}$ **c.** $\frac{2}{10}$ **d.** $\frac{4}{10}$ **e.** $\frac{6}{10}$

ANSWERS: a .8 b .1 c .2 d .4 e .6

Some decimals are fractions with **100** in their **denominators**.

EXAMPLE: $\frac{1}{100} = .01$

These decimals have **two places**. They are called **hundredths**.

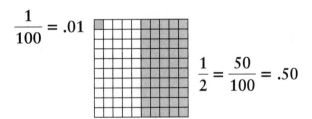

$$\frac{1}{100} = .01 \qquad \frac{1}{2} = \frac{50}{100} = .50$$

Write these fractions as decimals.

EXAMPLE: $\frac{3}{10} = .03$

a. $\frac{8}{100}$ **b.** $\frac{12}{100}$ **c.** $\frac{20}{100}$ **d.** $\frac{40}{100}$ **e.** $\frac{60}{100}$

ANSWERS: a .08 b .12 c .20 d .40 e .60

Some decimals are fractions with **1000** in their **denominators**.

EXAMPLE: $\dfrac{1}{1000} = .001$

These decimals have **three places**. They are called **thousandths**.

$$\dfrac{4}{1000} = .004 \qquad \dfrac{69}{1000} = .069 \qquad \dfrac{252}{1000} = .252$$

Write these fractions as decimals.

EXAMPLE: $\dfrac{3}{1000} = .003$

a. $\dfrac{82}{1000}$ **b.** $\dfrac{125}{1000}$ **c.** $\dfrac{20}{1000}$ **d.** $\dfrac{4}{1000}$ **e.** $\dfrac{613}{1000}$

ANSWERS: a .082 b .125 c .020 d .004 e .613

You can write a whole number and a decimal together. The decimal point separates the whole number from the decimal.

$3\dfrac{1}{2} = 3\dfrac{5}{10} = 3.5$

$2\dfrac{3}{4} = 2\dfrac{75}{100} = 2.75$

Write the mixed numbers as decimals.

EXAMPLE: $1\dfrac{1}{2} = 1.5$

a. $5\dfrac{1}{4} =$ **b.** $2\dfrac{3}{4} =$ **c.** $1\dfrac{5}{100} =$

ANSWERS: a. 5.25 b. 2.75 c. 1.05

Name the decimal. Write the answer.

EXAMPLES

.5 = <u>5 tenths</u>   .05 = <u>5 hundredths</u>   .50 = <u>50 hundredths</u>   .005 = <u>5 thousandths</u>

---

a. .4 = **b.** .04 = **c.** .44 = **d.** .035 = **e.** .123 =

**ANSWERS: a. 4 tenths b. 4 hundredths c. 44 hundredths
d. 35 thousandths e. 123 thousandths**

Add and Subtract Decimals

You gave me $10.00. The total was $8.65. Your change is $1.35.

Remember: The decimal point separates whole numbers from decimals. Keep whole numbers together. Keep decimals together. The decimal point **does not move** when you add or subtract decimals.

EXAMPLES

Add the decimals.

3.5	2.17	6.003	22.6	← You can write →	22.60
+ 2.3	+ .34	+ 5.22	+ 5.37		+ 5.37
5.8	2.51	11.223	27.97		27.97

EXAMPLES

Subtract the decimals.

3.5	2.17	6.003	22.6	← You can write →	22.60
− 2.3	− .34	− 5.220	− 5.37		− 5.37
1.2	1.83	.783	17.23		17.23

Practice: Add or subtract.

a. 2.6   **b.** 8.38   **c.**   4.006   **d.** 72.5   **e.** 5.80   **f.** 23.092
    − 1.1   + .52   −2.61   + 9.04   +7.08   −10.515

Word Problems: Do you add or subtract? Write an estimate and an equation. Solve the problem.

EXAMPLE

Abram got paid **$37.55** his first week of work. He got paid **$23.65** his second week. He got paid **$46.75** his third week. How much did he get paid altogether?

ESTIMATE: $40 + $20 + $50 = $110

EQUATION: **$37.55 + $23.65 + $46.75 = $107.95**

Practice Problems

1. Melvin goes on a 3-day bike trip. He bikes 30.5 miles the first day, 34.6 miles the second day, and 42.8 miles the third day. How far does he ride?

   ESTIMATE: _____

   EQUATION: _____

2. The shop teacher buys a 48-inch strip of metal. He cuts off a piece 12.56 inches long. How much of the metal strip is left? *Remember:* You can write 48 as 48.00.

   ESTIMATE: _____

   EQUATION: _____

3. Ada weighs 116.5 pounds. Minka weighs 110.3 pounds. How much more does Ada weigh than Minka?

   ESTIMATE: _____

   EQUATION: _____

SEE PAGE 200 FOR ANSWERS.

Multiply and Divide Decimals

Multiply Decimals

Keys to Understanding

Multiply Decimals

Ten × Ones	= Tens	Tenths × Ones	= Tenths
10 × 2	= 20	.6 × 2	= 1.2
Ten × Tens	= Hundreds	Tenths × Tenths	= Hundredths
10 × 50	= 500	.6 × .6	= .36
Ten × Hundreds	= Thousands	Tenths × Hundredths	= Thousandths
10 × 300	= 3000	.6 × .30	= .180

EXAMPLES

3.5	4.1	2.7	1.04	2.37
× 5	× .4	× .42	× 3	× .5
17.5	1.64	1.134	3.12	1.185

Practice: Multiply the decimals. Write the answer.

a. 1.8
  × 6

b. 6.3
  × .5

c. 5.9
  × .37

d. 4.06
  × 6

e. 3.10
  ×.8

Word Problem: Answer the questions. Write an estimate and an equation.

EXAMPLE

Abram has a coupon for 55¢ off every movie ticket. He takes 3 friends to the movies. How much money does he save?

ESTIMATE: 3 × .60 = $1.80

EQUATION: 3 × .55 = $1.65

Practice Problem: Mike's fishing pole is in 4 pieces. Each piece is 1.3 feet long. How long is the whole pole?

SEE PAGE 200 FOR ANSWERS.

Key to Understanding

Divide Decimals

A **divisor** is the number that divides. $6 \div 3$ or $3\overline{)6}$

A **dividend** is the number being divided.

3 is the **divisor**.

6 is the **dividend**.

To divide a decimal:

Step A: Multiply to remove the decimal in the divisor. Multiply the divisor and the dividend by the same number.

HINT: Multiply a divisor with tenths by 10. Multiply a divisor with hundredths by 100.

$.25\overline{)5.075}$

$100 \times .25 = 25$
$100 \times 5.075 = 507.5$

Step B: Divide. Remember the decimal in the answer is above the decimal in the dividend.

$$\begin{array}{r} 20.3 \\ 25\overline{)507.5} \end{array}$$

Step C: Check. Multiply the answer by the divisor.

$.25 \times 20.3 = 5.075$

EXAMPLE $.4\overline{)48}$

ESTIMATE: How many $\dfrac{4}{10}$ are in **48**?

$\dfrac{4}{10}$ = about $\dfrac{1}{2}$

There are about a hundred $\dfrac{1}{2}$ in **48**.

EQUATION: $.4\overline{)48}$

Step A: Multiply the divisor and the dividend by 10.

$10 \times .4 = 4 \quad 10 \times 48 = 480$

Step B: Divide.

$4\overline{)480} = 120$

Step C: Check.

$.4 \times 120 = 48$

Strategies for Test-Taking Success: Math © Thomson Heinle.
Photocopying this page is prohibited by law.

Divide. Write the answer.

$$\begin{array}{r} 600 \\ .6\overline{)360} \end{array}$$

a. $.5\overline{)120}$ **b.** $.10\overline{)620}$ **c.** $.25\overline{)22.5}$ **d.** $.50\overline{)250}$

Word Problems: Do you add, subtract, multiply, or divide? Use the table below to answer the questions. Write an estimate and an equation. Solve the problem.

BREAKFAST MENU THEN AND NOW		
Food	**Cost in 1950**	**Cost Today**
Orange Juice	$ .15	$1.09
Milk	$ .10	$1.10
Two Eggs	$ .50	$1.58
Cereal	$ .20	$1.29
Fried Potatoes	$ .25	$1.19
Pancakes	$ .35	$3.99

EXAMPLE

How much are two eggs and fried potatoes today?

ESTIMATE: $1.60 + $1.00 = $2.60   EQUATION: $1.58 + $1.19 = $2.77

Practice Problems

1. Staziek buys breakfast for his family in 1950. He buys 3 orders of pancakes, 3 glasses of orange juice, and 3 glasses of milk. How much does he spend?

2. How much is the same breakfast today?

3. Today the waitress writes a bill for $5.25. She remembers she didn't bring the orange juice. She subtracts the cost of orange juice. How much is the bill?

4. Five friends all eat the same thing in 1950. The bill was $1.75. What did they eat?

SEE PAGE 201 FOR ANSWERS.

Percents

Percents describe **parts of a whole**.

A percent can be a **whole number**. 50% of 20 = **10**

A percent can be a **fraction**. 50% of 1 = $\frac{1}{2}$

A percent can be a **decimal**. 50% of .30 = **.15**

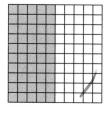

$$50\% = \frac{50}{100}$$

$$50\% \text{ of } 20 = 10$$

Percents compare **parts of a hundred** to **parts of a whole**.

$$\frac{\text{parts}}{\text{hundred}} = \frac{\text{parts}}{\text{whole}}$$

$$\frac{50}{100} = \frac{10}{20}$$

$$50\% \text{ of } 20 = 10$$

IMPORTANT PERCENTS	
1% of a number EXAMPLE: $\dfrac{1}{100} = \dfrac{4.2}{420}$	1% of 420 = 4.2 $1\% = \dfrac{1}{100} \times 420$ $1\% = .01 \times 420$
10% of a number EXAMPLE: $\dfrac{10}{100} = \dfrac{42}{420}$	10% of 420 = 42 10% of 420 $= \dfrac{1}{10} \times 420$ 10% of 420 $= .10 \times 420$
25% of a number EXAMPLE: $\dfrac{25}{100} = \dfrac{105}{420}$	25% of 420 = 105 25% of 420 $= \dfrac{1}{4} \times 420$ 25% of 420 $= .25 \times 420$
50% of a number EXAMPLE: $\dfrac{50}{100} = \dfrac{210}{420}$	50% of 420 = 210 50% of 420 $= \dfrac{1}{2} \times 420$ 50% of 420 $= .50 \times 420$

Find the Part, the Percent, or the Whole

$$\frac{\text{parts}}{\text{hundred}} = \frac{\text{parts}}{\text{whole}}$$

1. Multiply the **denominator** of one fraction by the **numerator** of the other fraction.
2. Divide that answer by the third number.

What is 60% of 20? $\dfrac{60}{100} \; \dfrac{?}{20}$ $60 \times 20 = 1200$

$1200 \div 100 = 12$
12 is 60% of 20.

12 is 60% of what number? $\dfrac{60}{100} \; \dfrac{12}{?}$ $12 \times 100 = 1200$

$1200 \div 60 = 20$
12 is 60% of 20.

12 is what % of 20? $\dfrac{?}{100} \; \dfrac{12}{20}$ $12 \times 100 = 1200$

$1200 \div 20 = 60$
60% of 20 is 12.

TIP

Remember:
change 60% to .60

Understand Word Problems with Percents

EXAMPLE A

Karl's math test has **45** problems. He gets **80%** of the problems correct. How many problems does he get correct?

ESTIMATE: 10% of 40 = 4

          80% = 8 × 10%

          80% of 40 = 8 × 4 = 32

EQUATION: $\dfrac{\text{part}}{\text{hundred}} = \dfrac{\text{part}}{\text{whole}}$ $\dfrac{80}{100} = \dfrac{?}{45}$

80 × 45 = 3600

3600 ÷ 100 = 36 correct answers

EXAMPLE B

Cindy has **60** chocolate hearts. She eats **12** of them. What percent of the total does she eat?

ESTIMATE: $\dfrac{10}{60} = \dfrac{1}{6} = 16.6\%$

EQUATION: $\dfrac{\text{part}}{\text{hundred}} = \dfrac{\text{part}}{\text{whole}}$ $\dfrac{?}{100} = \dfrac{12}{60}$

12 × 100 = 1200

1200 ÷ 60 = 20%

She eats 20 % of the hearts.

EXAMPLE C

14 kids in Woodland High School are absent on Monday. 14 is **5%** of the total number of kids at Woodland. How many kids go to Woodland?

ESTIMATE: 5% = 14

          10% = 28

          100% = 280

EQUATION: $\dfrac{\text{part}}{\text{hundred}} = \dfrac{\text{part}}{\text{whole}}$ $\dfrac{5}{100} = \dfrac{14}{?}$

14 × 100 = 1400

1400 ÷ 5 = 280

280 students go to Woodland High School.

Word Problems: Find a part, the percent, or the whole.

EXAMPLE

A dress is **30%** off. It's original price is **$125**. What is the sale price?

ESTIMATE: 10% of $125 = $12.50   30% is about $36 $125 − $36 is about $90.00

EQUATION: $\dfrac{30}{100} = \dfrac{?}{125}$ 30 × 125 = 3750   3750 ÷ 100 = 37.50

$125 − $37.50 = $87.50

Practice Problems

1. John buys a pair of jeans on sale for $36. They are usually $45. What percent does he save?

   ESTIMATE: _____

   EQUATION: _____

2. Costas plays basketball. Today, he makes 82% or 41 of his shots. How many shots does he make?

   ESTIMATE: _____

   EQUATION: _____

3. There are 125 fish in the pond. Carlos catches 10 of them. What percent does he catch?

   ESTIMATE: _____

   EQUATION: _____

4. Abby puts 6 cupcakes in her lunch bag. Her mother says, "Put some cupcakes back, Abby. You can't take 50% of the cupcakes I baked." How many cupcakes did her mother bake?

   ESTIMATE: _____

   EQUATION: _____

SEE PAGE 201 FOR ANSWERS.

Now, use your skills with fractions, decimals, and percents to take a Review Test.

CHAPTER 3: REVIEW TEST

Mark your answers on the Answer Grid.

1   **Pick the fraction. Fifteen minutes is a quarter of an hour.**

   A   1/25

   B   1/15

   C   1/4

   D   1/2

2   **Pick the biggest fraction.**

   A   2/4

   B   3/4

   C   4/8

   D   4/5

3   **The directions say: "Go 1/4 of a mile to the first stop light. Then go 2/4 of a mile to the corner." How far do you go altogether?**

   A   3/8 of a mile

   B   1/2 of a mile

   C   3/4 of a mile

   D   4/4 of a mile

4   **Samuel and Chris measure their feet. Samuel's foot is 11 5/6 inches long. Chris's foot is 11 3/6 inches long. How much shorter is Chris's foot?**

   A   2/6 of an inch shorter

   B   8/6 of an inch shorter

   C   2/12 of an inch shorter

   D   2 inches shorter

5   **There are 8 tablespoons in a stick of butter. How many teaspoons are in one stick of butter?**

> **1 teaspoon = 1/3 of a tablespoon**

   A   3/8

   B   1 8/3

   C   2 2/3

   D   24

6   **Sheila eats 1/2 of a box of brownies. Amy eats 1/2 as much. How much does Amy eat?**

   A   1 box

   B   1/4 of a box

   C   2/2 box

   D   1 1/2 boxes

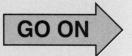

GO ON

7 Choose the answer with equivalent fractions.

A 2/3, 4/6, 10/15

B 1/5, 3/5, 4/5

C 2/3, 2/4, 2/5

D 1/2, 4/8, 6/3

8 Which fraction is equal to one?

A 1/2

B 3/3

C 4/2

D 5/4

9 Joleen is lost. She walks 1/2 mile in one direction. Then, she walks 1/4 of a mile in another direction. How far does she walk altogether?

A 2/6 of a mile

B 2/8 of a mile

C 2/4 of a mile

D 3/4 of a mile

10 Anatoly works 3 1/4 hours on Friday. He works 5 3/4 hours on Saturday. How many more hours does he work on Saturday than on Friday? Simplify the answer.

A 1 1/2 hours

B 2 2/4 hours

C 2 1/2 hours

D 9 hours

11 Simplify the fraction 4/8.

A 2/3

B 1/2

C 1/4

D 1/8

12 Convert 5/4 to its simplest form.

A 4/5

B 5 1/4

C 1 1/4

D 4 1/5

GO ON

13 Write the fractions as decimals.

3/10 3/100 3/1000

A .03, .003, .0003

B .3, .03, .003

C 3, 30, 300

D 3, 3.0, 3.00

14 Which decimal is equal to 3 1/2?

A 3.25

B 3.5

C 3.55

D .350

15 Add the times to find how fast the relay team swims altogether.

Boys Swim Team Relay Times in Seconds	
Luis	22.93
Chris	26.66
Alan	26.38
Jose	25.36

A 1.0133 seconds

B 10.133 seconds

C 101.33 seconds

D 1013.3 seconds

16 A board is 13.50 inches long. Eleni cuts off 2.25 inches. How long is the board now?

A .1150 inch

B 11 inches

C 11.25 inches

D 15.75 inches

17 Oskar buys four tickets for the dance. He pays $13.99 for each ticket. How much does he pay altogether?

A $27.98

B $55.00

C $55.96

D $139.90

18 Alicia sews buttons on her shirt. The front of the shirt is 14.4 inches long. She sews on 4 buttons. How far apart is each button?

A .36 inch

B 3.6 inches

C 10.4 inches

D 18.4 inches

GO ON

19 Andy walks 36.6 miles with his mother to earn money for charity. They walk 12.2 miles a day. How many days do they walk?

A   2.5 days

B   3 days

C   3.2 days

D   3.5 days

20 The sign says 25% off. The shoes are $68.00. How much do the shoes cost on sale?

A $6.80

B $17.00

C $43.00

D $51.00

21 There are 35 kids in the class. 21 of them get A's on the test. What percent get A's?

A   14%

B   25%

C   51%

D   60%

22 75%, or 42 kids, say that pizza is their favorite food on a date. How many kids are asked?

A   42 kids

B   50 kids

C   56 kids

D   75 kids

23 Four girls take turns playing a computer game. Each turn is the same number of minutes. They play for 48 minutes altogether. How long does each girl play?

A   .08 minutes

B   1.2 minutes

C   12 minutes

D   192 minutes

24 The bill is $13.60. Mark multiplies that amount by 15% for the tip. How much is the tip?

A $.204

B $2.04

C $2.044

D $20.40

**STOP. THIS IS THE END OF THE REVIEW TEST.
SEE PAGE 202 FOR ANSWERS**

STOP

Strategies for Test-Taking Success: Math © Thomson Heinle. Photocopying this page is prohibited by law.

...bra

...Work with Positive and Negative Numbers

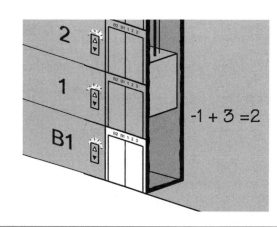

$-1 + 3 = 2$

TIP

Positive numbers are more than 0.

Negative numbers are less than 0.

Sam the Elevator Man: Add and Subtract Negative Numbers

A woman and a dog enter the elevator on the main floor.	0
1st trip Sam takes them up two floors.	$0 + 2 = 2$
2nd trip Then he goes down to the first basement.	$2 - 3 = -1$
3rd trip Sam picks up some boxes and takes them up to the main floor.	$-1 + 1 = 0$
4th trip The bell rings. A repairman is in the furnace room. The elevator goes down and gets him.	$0 - 2 = -2$
5th trip The bell rings again. It is the woman and her dog. He goes up to the second floor.	$-2 + 4 = 2$
6th trip Ten minutes later he takes them back to the main floor.	$2 - 2 = 0$
Sam's day is full of ups and downs!	

The Number Line

Negative direction ←

$$-6 \quad -5 \quad -4 \quad -3 \quad -2 \quad -1 \quad 0 \quad 1 \quad 2 \quad 3 \quad 4 \quad 5 \quad 6$$

→ **Positive direction**

Combine negative and positive numbers. Write the answer.

$$
\begin{array}{cccccc}
& \textbf{a.}\ -3 & \textbf{b.}\ 14 & \textbf{c.}\ -33 & \textbf{d.}\ 21 & \textbf{e.}\ 25 \\
4 & \underline{-4} & \underline{-5} & \underline{10} & \underline{-31} & \underline{-12} \\
\underline{-5} & & & & & \\
-1 & & & & &
\end{array}
$$

ANSWERS: a. −7   b. 9   c. −23   d. −10   e. 13

Word Problems: Write an estimate and an equation.

EXAMPLE

The thermometer says 2°. The temperature falls 5°. What does the thermometer say now?

←

$$-3° \quad -2° \quad -1° \quad 0° \quad 1° \quad 2°$$

ESTIMATE:

EQUATION: $2° - 5° = -3°$

Practice Problems

1. A submarine is 100 feet under the sea. It is at −100 feet. It goes down another 150 feet. How deep is it now?

   ESTIMATE: _____

   EQUATION: _____

2. Carlos plays cards. He wins 75 points. Then he loses 110 points. How many points does he have now?

   ESTIMATE: _____

   EQUATION: _____

SEE PAGE 203 FOR ANSWERS.

Multiply and Divide Negative Numbers

Problem

Van borrows $5 from his dad. Then he borrows another $5.

He borrows $5 two times. $-5 \times (+2) = -\$10$

Rule

To multiply or divide a positive number $(+)$ and a negative number $(-)$, the answer is a negative number $(-)$.

$$(+) \times (-) = - \qquad\qquad (+) \div (-) = -$$

$$\text{or} \qquad\qquad\qquad \text{or}$$

$$(-) \times (+) = - \qquad\qquad (-) \div (+) = -$$

Problem

Van makes $10 and takes it to his dad.

His dad says: *Keep your money.* His dad doesn't take the first $5. He doesn't take the second $5.

Van keeps $10. $-2 \times (-\$5) = +\$10$

Rule

To multiply or divide a negative number $(-)$ and a negative number $(-)$, the answer is a positive number $(+)$.

$$(-) \times (-) = + \qquad\qquad (-) \div (-) = +$$

Multiply or divide. Write the answer.

Example: $-5 \times 6 = -30$

a. $12 \times (-2)$ **b.** $-10 \times (-4)$ **c.** -3×5

d. $12 \div (-4)$ **e.** $-15 \div 5$ **f.** $-24 \div (-4)$

g. $-16 \div 4$

ANSWERS: a. −24   b. 40   c. −15   d. −3   e. −3   f. 6   g. −4

Word Problems: Do you multiply or divide? Write an estimate and an equation. Solve the problem.

EXAMPLE

A car goes 33 miles on a gallon of gas. It has 7 gallons in its gas tank. It goes 33 miles and then another 33 miles. How much gas does it have left?

ESTIMATE: The car uses 2 gallons. 7 gallons − 2 gallons is 5 gallons.

EQUATION: $2 \times (-1) = -2$ $\qquad$ $7 - 2 = 5$ gallons

TIP

With same signs (+ and + or − and −), the answer is positive (+).

With different signs (+ and − or − and +), the answer is negative (−).

Practice Problems

1. An elevator takes miners down to a gold mine. It goes 50 feet at a time. After 4 stops, how far down is the elevator?

   ESTIMATE: _____

   EQUATION: _____

2. Mrs. Garcia makes a budget. She writes a positive number for money she has. She writes a negative number for money she spends. She buys 3 sweaters for $43.25 each. What does she write?

   ESTIMATE: _____

   EQUATION: _____

3. It is 25° in Alaska. The temperature falls 8° every day. What is the temperature after 5 days?

   ESTIMATE: _____

   EQUATION: _____

4. Haile plays a game. Every time she loses, she gets −15 points. At the end of the evening, her score is −225. How many times does she lose?

   ESTIMATE: _____

   EQUATION: _____

SEE PAGE 203 FOR ANSWERS.

Check Your Answer

Juan buys 9 oranges. He makes orange juice with 3 oranges. How many oranges does he have left?	9 oranges − 3 oranges = 6 oranges $9 - 3 = 6$
Use addition to check subtraction.	**Check**: $6 + 3 = 9$
Juan puts 3 oranges on the table to make orange juice. He has 6 oranges still in the bag. How many oranges did he buy?	6 oranges + 3 oranges = 9 oranges $6 + 3 = 9$
Use subtraction to check addition.	**Check**: $9 - 3 = 6$
There are 100 blocks in Lin's town. 6 families live on each block. How many families live in the town?	100 blocks × 6 families = 600 families $100 \times 6 = 600$
Use division to check multiplication.	**Check**: $600 \div 6 = 100$
The 600 families in Lin's town each have a house. The town has 100 blocks. Each block has the same number of houses. How many houses are on each block in Lin's town?	600 houses ÷ 100 blocks = 6 houses $600 \div 100 = 6$
Use multiplication to check division.	**Check**: $6 \times 100 = 600$

Check your answer.

$6 + 12 = 18$ Check: $18 - 12 = 6$

a. $25 + 12 = 37$ Check:

b. $52 - 19 = 33$ Check:

c. $3 \times 17 = 51$ Check:

d. $64 \div 4 = 16$ Check:

ANSWERS: a. 37 − 12 = 25   b. 33 + 19 = 52
c. 51 ÷ 17 = 3   d. 16 × 4 = 64

Keys to Understanding

Variables

In algebra: Write letters (like *a*, *m*, *x*, or *y*) for numbers you don't know. These letters are called variables.

TIP

$+125 - 125 = 0$

"I weigh 125 pounds. How much does my dog weigh?"

---

dog's weight + Luisa's weight = 140 pounds

$$x \quad + \quad 125 \quad = \quad 140$$

Subtract her weight from both sides of the equation.

The dog weighs 15 pounds.

Check: 125 pounds + 15 pounds = 140 pounds

---

x = the dog's weight

$x + 125 = 140$ pounds

$x + 125 - 125 = 140 - 125$

$x + 0 = 15$

Find the price before the sale.	x = Price before sale
Price before sale − savings = Sale price	$x - \$3 = \$13$
Add the savings to both sides of the equation.	$x - \$3 + \$3 = \$13 + \$3$
The price before the sale is $16.	$x = \$16$
Check: $\$16 - \$3 = \$13$	

 ## Keys to Understanding

Solving an equation with one variable:

Add or subtract the **same** number to both sides of the equation. This does not change the equation.

$a + 4 = 12$	$s - 5 = 9$	$x + 43 = 137$	$y - 11 = 231$
$a + 4 - 4 = 12 - 4$	$s - 5 + 5 = 9 + 5$	$x + 43 - 43 = 137 - 43$	$y - 11 + 11 = 231 + 11$
$a = 8$	$s = 14$	$x = 94$	$y = 242$
Check: $8 + 4 = 12$	Check: $14 - 5 = 9$	Check: $94 + 43 = 137$	Check: $242 - 11 = 231$

Practice: Solve the equations with algebra. Find x or y.

Example: $x + 7 = 15$
$$x + 7 - 7 = 15 - 7$$
$$x = 8$$

a. $x - 15 = 7$ **b.** $y + 22 = 36$ **c.** $x - 16 = 54$

d. $y + 1/2 = 3 \ 1/2$ **e.** $x + .25 = 6.75$

Word Problems: Write an estimate and an equation. Solve the equation with algebra.

EXAMPLE

It is snowing. Bill drives slowly and carefully. He drives 11 miles under the speed limit. Bill drives 34 miles an hour. What is the speed limit?

ESTIMATE: about 44 miles an hour

EQUATION: $L - 11 = 34$
$$L = 45$$

Practice Problems

1. Carl sells greeting cards for his club. He charges $3.75 for a box. The club pays $2.25 for each box. What is the profit on each box?

   ESTIMATE: _____

   EQUATION: _____

2. Oklahoma City had 12.07 inches of rain in its wettest year. Oklahoma City already has 7.5 inches of rain this year. How much rain does Oklahoma City need to match the wettest year?

   ESTIMATE: _____

   EQUATION: _____

3. Maria is making a party mix with peanuts, raisins, chocolate candy, pretzels, and cereal. She wants to make 6 cups. She mixes 1/2 cup of peanuts, 1/2 cup of raisins, and 1/2 cup of chocolate candies. She adds 1 cup of pretzels. How many cups of cereal does she need to add?

   ESTIMATE: _____

   EQUATION: _____

SEE PAGE 204 FOR ANSWERS.

Strategies for Test-Taking Success: Math © Thomson Heinle. Photocopying this page is prohibited by law.

Multiply and Divide with Variables

Keys to Understanding

Ways to show multiplication and division:

Multiplication	Division
$3 \times y = 15$	$15 \div 3 = y$
$3y = 15$	$\dfrac{15}{3} = y$
$3(y) = 15$	$y = 3\overline{)15}$

TIP

Remember: $\dfrac{2}{2} = 1$

Laurie buys donuts for the baseball team. She buys 10 dozen donuts. How many people can have 2 donuts each?	
10 dozen = $10 \times 12 = 120$ donuts p = total people 120 donuts = donuts per person $\times$ total people	$120 = 2 \times p$
Divide both sides of the equation by 2.	$\dfrac{120}{2} = \dfrac{2p}{2}$
60 people can have 2 donuts each.	$60 = p$
Check: $120 = 2 \times 60$	

Multiply or divide. Find x or y. Write the answer.

Example: $4x = 36$

$$\frac{4x}{4} = \frac{36}{4}, x = 4$$

a. $5y = 125$ **b.** $10y = 2.50$ **c.** $5x = \dfrac{5}{4}$

d. $x \div 8 = 6$ **e.** $y \div 12 = 12$ **f.** $x \div .04 = 16$

g. $y \div 1/2 = 2$

ANSWERS: a. $y = 25$ b. $y = .25$ c. $x = 1/4$
d. $x = 48$ e. $y = 144$ f. $y = .64$ g. $y = 1$

Word Problems: Do you multiply or divide? Write an estimate and an equation. Use algebra to solve the equation.

EXAMPLE

Mila works 36 hours. Her check is $234. How much money does she make per hour?

ESTIMATE: $240 \div 40 = 6$ Mila makes about $6 an hour.

EQUATION: $36x = 234$

$$\frac{36}{36}x = \frac{234}{36} \qquad x = \$6.50$$

Practice Problems

1. Elona does 150 sit-ups in 10 minutes. How many sit-ups can she do in a minute?

   ESTIMATE: _____

   EQUATION: _____

2. Giovanni gets 28 phone calls from girls every week. How many calls does he get each day?

   ESTIMATE: _____

   EQUATION: _____

3. There are 315 minutes of class time in the school day. Each class plus the time between classes is 45 minutes. How many classes fit in the school day?

   ESTIMATE: _____

   EQUATION: _____

SEE PAGE 204 FOR ANSWERS.

Solve Algebra Problems

Keys to Understanding

Parentheses

Parentheses ( ) say: *Do the operations inside parentheses first.*

$$6\,(5 + 4) = x$$
$$6 \times 9 = x$$
$$54 = x$$

Substitute Numbers for Variables

A variable holds a place for a number.

To solve an equation: Substitute (put in) numbers for the variables.

Equation: $6s - 4p + 2 = x$

$s = 7\ p = 5$	$s = 10\ p = 3$
$6s - 4p + 2 = x$	$6s - 4p + 2 = x$
$6\,(7) - 4\,(5) + 2 = x$	$6(10) - 4(3) + 2 = x$
$42 - 20 + 2 = 24$	$60 - 12 + 2 = 50$

Substitute numbers for variables. Find the answer.

a. $y = 2$ What is $3y + 2y$?

b. $x = 5$ What is $3(x - 4) + 2x$?

c. $x = -2$ What is $4x + 5$?

d. $y = 1/4$ What is $4y + (y + 3/4)$?

ANSWERS: a. 10   b. 13   c. −3   d. 2

Some countries use Celsius degrees (C°) for temperature. Some countries use Fahrenheit degrees (F°).

22°C = 72°F

To change from Celsius to Fahrenheit: Use a formula, or general rule.

Celsius temperature = 5/9 (Fahrenheit temperature − 32 degrees)

$$C = 5/9 \ (F - 32)$$

What is 25° Celsius in Fahrenheit?

Step 1: Divide both sides of the equation by 5/9.

Step 2: Add 32 to both sides of the equation.

Step 3: 25° Celsius = 77° Fahrenheit

Check: 25 = 5/9 (77 − 32)

25 = 5/9 (45)

25 = 25

$$25° \ C = 5/9 \ (F - 32)$$

$$\frac{25}{5/9} = \frac{5/9}{5/9} \ (F - 32)$$

$$45 = F - 32$$

$$45 + 32 = F - 32 + 32$$

$$77 = F$$

TIP

A number over itself is 1.

$$\frac{9}{9} = 1 \qquad \frac{3/4}{3/4} = 1$$

Use a formula. Solve the problem.

1. The Celsius temperature is 5°. What is the temperature in Fahrenheit?

2. The formula to change inches to centimeters is:
   inches = centimeters × .39
   How many inches is 78 centimeters?

ANSWERS: 1. 41°   2. 30.4 inches

Strategies for Test-Taking Success: Math © Thomson Heinle. Photocopying this page is prohibited by law.

Julie draws a mathematical pattern.

Formulas are patterns.

Find the pattern. What is the next number?

$$2 \quad 4 \quad 8 \quad ?$$

Think: How do I go from one number to the next number?
Do I add, subtract, multiply, or divide?

$$2 \times 2 = 4 \qquad\qquad 2 \times 4 = 8$$

The pattern is $2x$. The next number is 16.

Find the pattern.

1. 2   7   17   37

2. 2   5   14   51

ANSWERS: 1. $2x + 3$ 2. $3x - 1$

Choose the Correct Equation

Equations are patterns. Use patterns to solve problems.

Look at the problem. Choose the right equation.

Emilio walks half as fast as his father. How fast does Emilio walk?
E = Emilio; F = Father

$E = 1/2\ F$ $\qquad\qquad$ $E = 2F$ $\qquad\qquad$ $E = F + 2$

Think: 1/2 as fast means $1/2 \times$ father's speed
Choose: $E = 1/2\ F$

Choose the correct equation.

1. It costs $7.25 a pound plus $3.00 to send a package to Italy.
   Which is the correct equation for the cost of a package to Italy?

   p = number of pounds

   a. cost $= 3p + 7.25$ **b.** cost $= 7.25p + 3$ **c.** cost $= \dfrac{p}{3} + 7.25$

2. A man drives home. He drives 40 miles in an hour. Which is the
   correct equation for the distance he travels?

   h = hours

   a. distance $= \dfrac{40}{h}$ **b.** distance $= 40h$ **c.** distance $= 40 + h$

ANSWERS: 1. a   2. b

Inequalities

TIP

< and > always point to the **smaller** number. **x < 8** means that x can be any number before **8**, but not 8. **x > 8** means that x can be any number after, 8 but not 8.

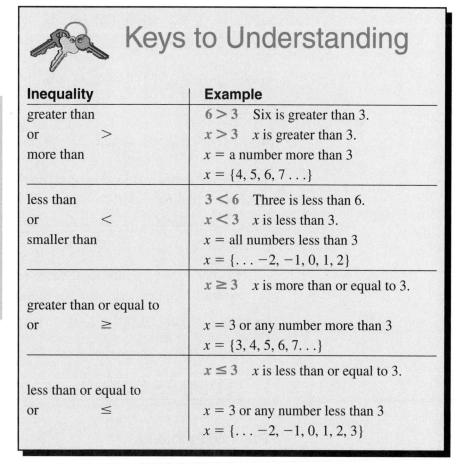

Keys to Understanding

Inequality	Example
greater than or > more than	$6 > 3$ Six is greater than 3. $x > 3$ x is greater than 3. x = a number more than 3 $x = \{4, 5, 6, 7 \ldots\}$
less than or < smaller than	$3 < 6$ Three is less than 6. $x < 3$ x is less than 3. x = all numbers less than 3 $x = \{\ldots -2, -1, 0, 1, 2\}$
greater than or equal to or ≥	$x \geq 3$ x is more than or equal to 3. x = 3 or any number more than 3 $x = \{3, 4, 5, 6, 7 \ldots\}$
less than or equal to or ≤	$x \leq 3$ x is less than or equal to 3. x = 3 or any number less than 3 $x = \{\ldots -2, -1, 0, 1, 2, 3\}$

Inequalities: The Curfew	
Tom wants to go to a concert. He says, "I'll come home at midnight."	$x = 12$
"No, you won't," says his father. "You can come home home earlier, at 8:00, 9:00, 10:00, or 11:00, but you can't come home at midnight."	$x < 12$
"Please?" asks Tom. "The concert ends at 11:30. I can't leave before it's over!"	
"Well, all right," says his father. "You can come home at midnight or earlier, but not one minute later."	$x \leq 12$

Practice: Match the inequality to the numbers.

1. $x < 4 =$

   a. $\{\ldots -3, -2, -1, 0, 1, 2, 3\}$ **b.** $\{\ldots 2, 3, 4\}$ **c.** $\{5, 6, 7 \ldots\}$

2. $x \leq 4 =$

   a. $\{\ldots -3, -2, -1, 0, 1, 2, 3\}$ **b.** $\{\ldots 2, 3, 4\}$ **c.** $\{5, 6, 7 \ldots\}$

3. $x > 4 =$

   a. $\{\ldots -3, -2, -1, 0, 1, 2, 3\}$ **b.** $\{\ldots 2, 3, 4\}$ **c.** $\{5, 6, 7 \ldots\}$

Word Problems: How do you write the number? Choose the correct inequality.

EXAMPLE

Redwoods are very old trees. Some redwoods are 2,000 or more years old. You can write the age of these redwoods as:

a. $R = 2,000$ **b.** $R < 2,000$ **c.** $R > 2,000$ **d.** $R \geq 2,000$

Think: **2,000 or more** means 2,000 or numbers greater than 2,000.

The answer is d. $R \geq 2,000$

Practice Problems

1. Some animals are disappearing from the earth. There are fewer than 8,000 tigers in the world. You can write this number as:

   a. $T = 8,000$ **b.** $T < 8,000$ **c.** $T > 8,000$ **d.** $T \leq 8,000$

2. There are two numbers, x and y. x is 3 less than y or equal to y. You can write this as:

   a. $x = y - 3$ **b.** $x = y + 3$ **c.** $x \leq y - 3$ **d.** $x \geq y + 3$

SEE PAGE 204 FOR ANSWERS.

Strategies for Test-Taking Success: Math © Thomson Heinle. Photocopying this page is prohibited by law.

Try Different Strategies to Solve Problems

1. **Estimate and check**

   A cookie recipe uses 3/4 cup of milk. The school cook makes 12 batches of cookies. How much milk does he use?

ESTIMATE:	EQUATION:
He will need < 10 cups because $3/4 < 1$. Maybe he will need about 10 cups. Does $3/4 \times 12 = 10$?	$\dfrac{3}{4} \times 12 = \dfrac{36}{4} = 9$ The cook uses 9 cups of milk.

2. **Use a simpler example**

   The restaurant serves 396 people every day. 1/3 of them have pie. How many have pie?

Make a problem with small numbers.
Try to add, subtract, multiply, or divide.

If 6 people are at the restaurant and $\dfrac{1}{3}$ have pie, then $\dfrac{1}{3}$ of $6 = 2$.

$6 + \dfrac{1}{3} = 6\dfrac{1}{3}$ That is not right. I do not add.

$6 \div \dfrac{1}{3} = 18$ That is not right. I do not divide.

$6 \times \dfrac{1}{3} = 2$ That is right. I can multiply to get the right answer.

$396 \times \dfrac{1}{3} = \dfrac{396}{3} = 132$

132 people eat pie.

3. **Work backwards**

Jennifer gets $100 for her birthday. She buys a sweater for $42. Then she buys two CDs. They each cost the same price. She has $22 left. How much is each CD?

To work backwards:	
Subtract the sweater price.	$100 - 42 = 58$
Subtract the $22 she has left.	$58 - 22 = 36$
She buys 2 CDs. Divide 36 by 2.	$36 \div 2 = 18$
Jennifer spends $18 on each CD.	

4. **Draw a solution**

Alexandra can't find her new gloves. She decides to look for them. She walks .50 mile to school, .30 mile to her friend's house, .50 mile to the hamburger place, and .75 mile back home. How far does she walk? (Her gloves are at home!)

Alexandra's Walk

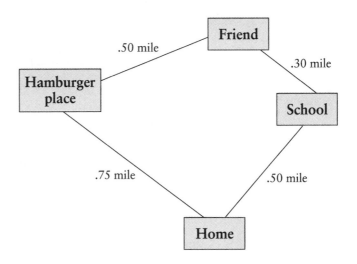

Alexandra walks .50 + .30 + .50 + .75 mile.
She walks 2.05 miles.

Word Problems: Practice the problem-solving strategies. Use your own paper.

Practice Problems

1. A man gives 1/5 of his paintings, or 12 paintings, to his son. He gives 1/4 of his paintings to his neighbor. He gives 1/3 of his paintings to the museum. How many of his paintings does he keep?

   Draw a solution.

2. Mike thinks it will take two hours to do his homework. Two hours is 120 minutes. He works on English for 45 minutes, on math for 30 minutes, and on science for 20 minutes. How much time does he have left?

   Work backwards.

3. There is a 40% off sale at Peter's Department Store. John wants a jacket that costs $59.95. What is the sale price of the jacket?

   Use simpler numbers.

4. One serving of cereal is 3/4 of a cup. There are 10 1/2 cups of cereal in the box. How many servings are in the box of cereal?

   Estimate and check.

SEE PAGE 204 FOR ANSWERS.

Now, use your algebra skills to take a Review Test.

CHAPTER 4: REVIEW TEST

Mark your answers on the Answer Grid.

1 You can run a mile in 7 minutes 45 seconds. You want to run a 7-minute mile. How close are you to your goal?

A −15 seconds

B −45 seconds

C +45 seconds

D +1 minute 15 seconds

2 The thermometer says −3° at five o'clock. Two hours later, the thermometer says −7°. What is the change in temperature?

A −12

B −7

C −4

D +4

3 A submarine is −30 feet below sea level. It goes down 10 feet four more times. Now how far below sea level is the submarine?

A −70 feet

B −40 feet

C −34 feet

D −20 feet

4 Central High School's basketball team has had the same record for 5 years. Their total wins are 75 games. Their total loses are 50 games. What is the team's record each year?

A +12 −12

B +15 −10

C +25 −25

D +75 −50

5 Solve this equation:
$-4\,(-12) =$

A −48

B −16

C 16

D 48

6 Solve this equation:
$-12 \div -4 =$

A −3

B −16

C 3

D 48

GO ON

7 The coupon says: "Spend $25. Get $5 off." You have two coupons. Your bill is $50. What do you pay?

A $x = \$60 - \$5 = \$55$

B $x = \$50 - 2(\$5) = \$40$

C $x = \$2(25) - \$15 = \$35$

D $x = \$25 - \$10 = \$15$

8 You have 5 classes. You need 2 notebooks for each class. You also need 3 extra notebooks. Your bill is $26.00. Which equation shows how much each notebook costs?

A $\$26.00 = 10x + 3x$

B $\$26.00 = 10x + 3$

C $\$26.00 = 10x - \$2.60$

D $\$26.00 = \$26.00 - \$8.00$

9 A car goes 22 miles on a gallon of gas. How many miles does it go on 10 gallons?

A 2.2 miles

B 32 miles

C 200 miles

D 220 miles

10 George drives his friend, Carl, to school every day. After school, he drives Carl home. George drives 12 miles a day. Carl lives 1.5 miles on the other side of the school. How far is the school from George's house?

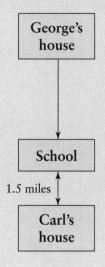

A 5 miles

B 4 miles

C 3 miles

D 2 miles

11 $m = 5, n = 3$
Solve the equation:
$C = 1/2\, m + n$

A 4

B 5 1/2

C 6 1/2

D 13

GO ON

Strategies for Test-Taking Success: Math © Thomson Heinle. Photocopying this page is prohibited by law.

12 Solve the equation:
$x = 7, y = 5$ $z = 3(x + y)$

A 15

B 22

C 26

D 36

13 How many centimeters is 13 inches?
Use the formula:
inches = centimeters × .39

A 12.87

B 32.61

C 33.33

D 84.61

14 The Celsius temperature = $-10°$.
What is the Fahrenheit temperature?
Use the formula:
$C = 5/9 \, (F - 32)$

A .20° F

B 14° F

C 22° F

D 26.4° F

15 Look for a pattern. What is the fifth number?

2, 4 1/2, 7, 9 1/2,

A 10 1/2

B 11

C 12

D 12 1/2

16 Look for a pattern. What is the fifth number?

3, 13, 33, 63,

A 73

B 96

C 93

D 103

17 Barbara's mother orders two pairs of sneakers on the Internet. Her bill is $75.00. The bill includes $5.00 for shipping. How much is each pair of shoes? Choose the correct equation.

A $75 = 2x + 5$

B $75 = 2x - 5$

C $x = 75 + 5$

D $x = 5 \, (75 + x)$

GO ON

18 Silvio takes the bus to the library on Saturday. Sometimes he gets there in 30 minutes. Sometimes it takes him longer to get there. Choose the inequality that describes how long it takes Silvio to go to the library.

A $y < 30$ minutes

B $y > 30$ minutes

C $y \leq 30$ minutes

D $y \geq 30$ minutes

19 Match the inequality to the number. $x > 10$

A $\{10, 11, 12, 13, \ldots\}$

B $\{11, 12, 13, 14, \ldots\}$

C $\{\ldots, 6, 7, 8, 9, 10\}$

D $\{\ldots, 5, 6, 7, 8, 9, \ldots\}$

20 The coldest day in March is 23°. The warmest day is 64°. Which inequalities show the temperatures in March?

A $x > 23$ and $x < 64$

B $x \geq 23$ and $x \leq 64$

C $x < 23$ and $x > 64$

D $x \leq 23$ and $x \geq 64$

21 Olga and her three friends make friendship bracelets. They need 15 beads for each bracelet. Olga wants to know how many beads she needs to buy. She multiplies 15 beads × 4 bracelets. Her answer is 60 beads. How can she check her answer?

A $60 \times 4 = 240$

B $60 + 4 = 64$

C $60 \div 4 = 15$

D $60 - 4 = 56$

22 Each of Olga's friendship bracelets has 4 yellow beads and 6 blue beads. The rest are red beads. Olga adds the yellow and blue beads. She gets 10 beads. Then, she subtracts the 10 beads from the 15 beads on each bracelet: $15 - 10 = 5$. She thinks she needs 5 red beads. How can she check her answer?

A $4 \times 6 = 24$

B $6 + 5 = 11$

C $15 \div 5 = 3$

D $5 + 10 = 15$

STOP. THIS IS THE END OF THE REVIEW TEST.
SEE PAGE 205 FOR ANSWERS

Strategy 24   Ratios

ICE CREAM RATIOS

It is the end of the year. Ms. Raspberry takes her class to buy ice cream cones.

There are 25 kids in the class.	The whole class: **25/25** or **25:25**
11 kids get chocolate ice cream.	The ratio of chocolate lovers to the whole class: **11/25** or **11:25**
6 kids get vanilla ice cream.	The ratio of vanilla lovers to the whole class: **6/25** or **6:25**
4 kids get strawberry ice cream.	The ratio of strawberry lovers to the whole class: **4/25** or **4:25**
3 kids get Rocky Road ice cream.	The ratio of Rocky Road lovers to the whole class: **3/25** or **3:25**
Carlos gets lime sherbet.	The ratio of lime sherbet lovers to the whole class: **1/25** or **1:25**

Height Ratios

Ratio: big brother to father = 6:5.5

Ratio: little boy to big brother = 1:2

Ratio: baby to little boy = 2:3

baby: 2 feet   little boy: 3 feet   big brother: 6 feet   father: 5.5 feet

Keys to Understanding

Ratios

Ratios compare numbers.

I am 6 feet tall. My little brother is 3 feet tall.
The ratio of my height to my brother's height is **2** to **1**.

Write ratios:

in words	**two to one**	or **2 to 1**
like a fraction	**2/1**	
with two dots	**2:1**	

Circle the ratios.

a. 3:10   **b.** 3⟌10   **c.** 3/10
d. 3(10)   **e.** 3 and 10   **f.** 3 to 10

ANSWERS: a, c, and f are ratios.

Word Problems: Write each ratio in two ways.

EXAMPLE

The ratio of sunny days to snowy or rainy days in New York in February was 11 to 17.

<u>11 : 17</u>   <u>11/17</u>

Practice Problems

1. One in every six pets is a rabbit. The ratio of rabbits to other pets is 1 to 6.

2. There are 23 dark-haired people for every red-haired person. The ratio of dark-haired people to red-haired people is 23 to 1.

SEE PAGE 207 FOR ANSWERS.

Ratios Help Solve Problems

Find the number of boys and girls in a class of 30 students.
Use the ratio **3:2**.

Ratio: **three** boys to **two** girls   **3:2** or **3/2**

Like fractions:
  Multiply a ratio by one and
  the ratio stays the same.

$$\frac{2}{2} \times \frac{3}{2} = \frac{6}{4}$$

  the ratio 3/2 = the ratio 6/4

How many boys to how many girls = 30 students?

Use algebra. Multiply the ratio.

  $3x$ = boys
  $2x$ = girls

$3x + 2x = 30$
$5x = 30$
$x = 30/5$
$x = 6$

$3 \times 6 = 18$ boys
$2 \times 6 = 12$ girls

the ratio 3/2 = the ratio 18/12   18 boys + 12 girls = 30 students

Keys to Understanding

Build a Table

Question: John and his girlfriend go to a football game. They spend **$30** for tickets, **$4** for the bus ride, and **$20** for refreshments. How much do they spend altogether?

Title

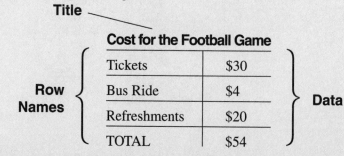

Cost for the Football Game

Row Names

Tickets	$30
Bus Ride	$4
Refreshments	$20
TOTAL	$54

Data

Use Tables to See Ratios

Ratio of boys to girls = 3:2			The title with a ratio
Class Size	**Boys**	**Girls**	The name of each column
15	9	6	The number of boys and girls in a class of 15 students
25	15	10	The number of boys and girls in a class of 25 students
30	18	12	The number of boys and girls in a class of 30 students

Practice: Use ratios to solve problems. Finish the table.

People in the United States like pets. They like dogs a little more than cats.
The ratio of pet cats to pet dogs is 8 to 9.

People with pets	People with cats	People with dogs
_17_	_8_	_9_
34	___	___
68	___	___

SEE PAGE 207 FOR ANSWERS.

Strategy 25

Probability

Use ratios to guess about the future. The ratio compares what happens **now** to what **can** happen. We call this **probability**.

EXAMPLE A

A penny has two sides. One side is called a **head**. The other side is called a **tail**.

Head   Tail

What is the probability that the penny lands with the **head side up**?
We throw a penny up 10 times and make a table. Here are the results:

WAYS A PENNY FALLS

Heads	Tails
卌	卌

The conclusion: A penny falls **1/2 of the time** with the **head** side up.
It falls **1/2 of the time** with the **tail** side up.

The probability that a penny will fall with the head side up is **1 to 2**.

EXAMPLE B

What is the probability that the penny lands with the **tail side up both times** in **two throws**?
Here are the results:

Probability of Two Tails in Two Throws

heads – heads	**tails – tails**
heads – tails	tails – heads

Two tails in **two throws** happens **1** out of **4** times.
Probability = **1/4**

EXAMPLE C

Samuel has **6** socks in the drawer: **2** white, **2** black, and **2** red.
He randomly pulls out a black sock.
What is the probability that he will pull out a second black sock?

We make a table.

B = black   W = white   R = red

Socks in the Sock Drawer

B He takes this sock.	B	W
W	R	R

He has **5** socks left in the drawer.
He has only **1** black sock in the drawer.
The probability that he will pick the black sock is **1/5**.

Word Problems: Write the probability.

Practice Problems

1. There are 10 pieces of paper in a jar at the school fair. The pieces of paper are numbered 1, 2, 3, 4, 5, 6, 7, 8, 9, and 10. What is the probability that you will pick number 9?

2. You have a quarter, a dime, and a penny in a box. You reach in the box and pick up the penny. You reach in the box again and randomly pick a second coin. What is the probability that you will pick up the quarter?

3. It always rains ten days this month. There are 30 days in this month. What is the probability that it will rain today?

SEE PAGE 207 FOR ANSWERS.

Graphs

Graphs have pictures, lines, and numbers to help you understand information.

Keys to Understanding

Graphs

Data	Annie gets these scores on her math tests: 95, 83, 99, 81, 90	95, 83, 99, 81, and 90 are **data**.
Conclusion	Gabe's best swimming time for the 50-meter freestyle is 1 minute and 3 seconds.	**Conclusion:** Gabe cannot swim the 50-meter freestyle faster than 1 minute and 3 seconds.
Display	We display information on a graph.	**Display** means *show*.
Label	The label says: "Minutes spent on the telephone."	The **labels** on the graph *name* the data.
Results	Ali and Derrick race three times. Ali wins one time and Derrick wins two times.	**Results:** Ali: 1 win Derrick: 2 wins
Key	Look in the key to understand the graph.	The **key** shows what the shapes and colors on the graph mean.

Write words from the word box on the correct line.

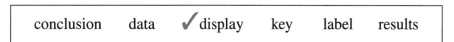

conclusion   data   ✓ display   key   label   results

display

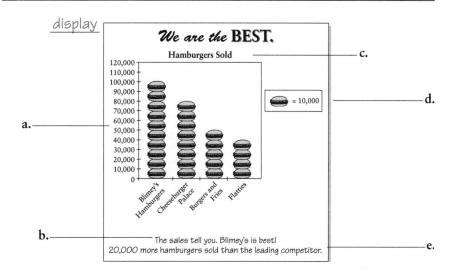

We are the BEST.

Hamburgers Sold — c.

🍔 = 10,000 — d.

a.

b.

The sales tell you. Blimey's is best!
20,000 more hamburgers sold than the leading competitor. — e.

SEE PAGE 207 FOR ANSWERS.

Circle Graphs

Circle graphs compare the **parts** of a **whole**.
This circle graph compares how Peter spends his money every week.

The title tells us that the whole circle is $23. The circle pieces are the parts.	
His telephone cost piece is white. It is small.	Peter spends $2 on his telephone every week.
The food cost piece is blue. It is large.	Peter spends $10 on food every week.

Peter's Budget: $23 a Week

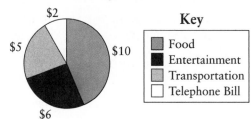

Key
- Food
- Entertainment
- Transportation
- Telephone Bill

Check the best answer.

> **EXAMPLE**
>
> The **key** shows:
>
> **a.** ___ data   **b.** ✓ labels   **c.** ___ labels and data

1. How much money does Peter spend a week?

   a. ___ $23   **b.** ___ $10   **c.** ___ $6   **d.** ___ $16

2. How much money does Peter spend on transportation a week?

   a. ___ $5   **b.** ___ $10   **c.** ___ $6   **d.** ___ $2

3. How much money does Peter spend on food and entertainment a week?

   a. ___ $10   **b.** ___ $5   **c.** ___ $16   **d.** ___ $25

ANSWERS: 1. a 2. a 3. c

Bar Graphs

Bar graphs compare separate things.
This bar graph compares the calories in different drinks.

The drink names are on the **horizontal**←→ **axis** (line).	Find the name of the drink.
The calorie data is on the **vertical** axis (line).	Look at the bar above the name. **Read across from the vertical axis to the top of the bar.**
6 ounces of orange juice = 90 calories	Find the calories in that drink.

Calories in a 6-Ounce Drink

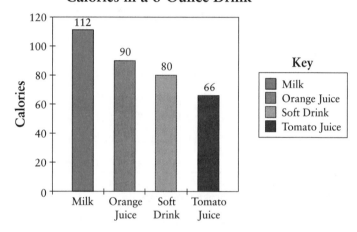

Check the best answer.

> **EXAMPLE**
>
> This horizontal axis has:
>
> **a.** ___ data   **b.** ✓ labels

1. This vertical axis has

   a. ___ data   **b.** ___ labels
   c. ___ data and a label **d.** ___ drinks

2. Milk has how many calories?

   a. ___ 66   **b.** ___ 80   **c.** ___ 90   **d.** ___ 112

3. A soft drink has how many fewer calories than milk?

   a. ___ 192   **b.** ___ 90   **c.** ___ 80   **d.** ___ 32

ANSWERS: 1. c 2. d 3. d

Scatterplots compare many small pieces of data.
To make a scatterplot: Go up from the horizontal axis. Go across from the vertical axis. Make a dot.

Jorge says it rains more when it is hotter. Alex does not agree. They make a scatterplot of temperatures and rain amounts for 11 days.

Then they make a line of best fit. A line of best fit is a line that comes closest to the most points.

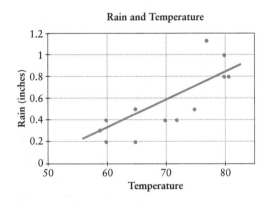

Rain and Temperature

Check the best answer.

EXAMPLE

The scatterplot shows that there are more inches of rain if temperatures

a. ✔ are high   **b.** ___ are low   **c.** ___ do not matter

---

1. The line of best fit

   a. ___ touches every point   **b.** ___ cannot touch points
   c. ___ is close to the most points

2. How many days is the temperature close to 60 degrees?

   a. ___ 1   **b.** ___ 2   **c.** ___ 3

3. How many inches does it rain on the rainiest day?

   a. ___ .4   **b.** ___ .8   **c.** ___ 1.15

ANSWERS: 1. c 2. c 3. c

Strategies for Test-Taking Success: Math © Thomson Heinle. Photocopying this page is prohibited by law.

A **line graph** shows changes across **time** or **distance**.
Alicia records her running time on a chart for two months. Then she makes a line graph.

Date	Time (in seconds)
March 1	17.3
March 8	17.1
March 15	16.2
March 22	16.4
March 29	15.2
April 5	15.3
April 12	14.2
April 19	14.5

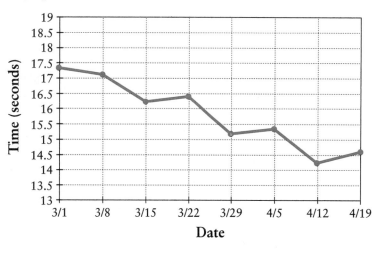

Check the best answer.

EXAMPLE

How many seconds faster does Alicia run on April 19th than on March 1st?

a. ✓ about 3 seconds faster   **b.** ___ about 2 seconds faster   **c.** ___ about 1 second faster

1. The line graph shows that:

   a. ___ Alicia runs faster in April than in March.
   b. ___ Alicia runs slower in April than in March.
   c. ___ Alicia runs the same rate in March and April.

2. What is a good description of Alicia's times?

   a. ___ She runs faster in each race.
   b. ___ She runs faster for a few races, then slows down, and then runs faster again.
   c. ___ She runs more slowly in April than in March.

3. What day did Alicia have her fastest time?

   a. ___ March 1st   **b.** ___ April 12th   **c.** ___ April 19th

ANSWERS: 1. a 2. b 3. b

Keys to Understanding

x-axis	Name of the horizontal axis on the coordinate grid
y-axis	Name of the vertical axis on the coordinate grid
Interval	The space between two numbers on an axis The interval in the graph below is 2.
Scale	The numbers on the graph and the intervals between them The scale on the horizontal axis of this graph is from -8 to $+8$. The scale on the vertical axis of this graph is from -12 to $+12$.
Quadrant 1	We divide the coordinate grid into four parts. We call the parts quadrants. In Quadrant 1, *x* and *y* are positive.
Quadrant 2	In Quadrant 2, *x* is negative and *y* is positive.
Quadrant 3	In Quadrant 3, *x* and *y* are negative.
Quadrant 4	In Quadrant 4, *x* is positive and *y* is negative.

Quadrants

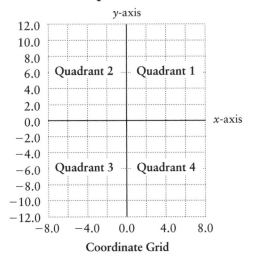

Coordinate Grid

You can draw equations on a graph.

EXAMPLE A

$y = 2x + 3$

Make a table of the equation. Choose some numbers for x.
Solve for each y. Get a y for each x.
Put the numbers for each x and y in the table.

If $x = 2$	If $x = 3$	If $x = 0$	If $x = -1$
$y = 2(2) + 3 = 7$	$y = 2(3) + 3 = 9$	$y = 2(0) + 3 = 3$	$y = 2(-1) + 3 = 1$

x	y
2	7
3	9
0	3
−1	1

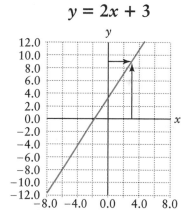

$y = 2x + 3$

To put the x and y values in the coordinate grid:

- Find the x-value on the x-axis. Go up, . . .

- Find the y-value on the y-axis. Go across, . . .

- Put a dot where the x-value and the y-value meet.

- Do this for all the x and y values.

- Draw a line that connects the dots.

Check the best answer.

EXAMPLE

If $x = 2$, then $y =$

a. ___ 2   **b.** ___ 3   **c.** ✓ 7   **d.** ___ 9

1. The line crosses the y-axis where $y =$

   a. ___ 2   **b.** ___ 5   **c.** ___ 3   **d.** ___ −5

2. If $x = -2$, then $y =$

   a. ___ −1   **b.** ___ 7   **c.** ___ 0   **d.** ___ −7

ANSWERS: 1. c 2. a

EXAMPLE B

$y = -2x - 1$

Make a table of the equation. Choose some numbers for x.
Solve for each y. Get a y for each x.
Put the numbers for each x and y into the table.

If $x = 2$	If $x = 0$	If $x = -2$
$y = -2(2) - 1 = -5$	$y = -2(0) - 1 = -1$	$y = -2(-2) - 1 = 3$

x	y	Quadrant
2	−5	4
0	−1	y-axis
−2	3	2

$y = -2x - 1$

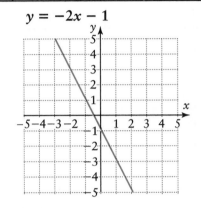

Look at the table in Example B. Check the best answer.

TIP

Remember:

Quadrant 1 = +x and +y

Quadrant 2 = −x and +y

Quadrant 3 = −x and −y

Quadrant 4 = +x and −y

EXAMPLE

If $x = 2$, then $y =$

a. ___ −2   **b.** ___ 0   **c.** ___ 4   **d.** ✔ −5

1. As x in this equation gets larger,

   a. ___ y gets smaller   **b.** ___ y = 3
   c. ___ y stays the same   **d.** ___ y = 0

2. How many x's are in Quadrant 1 in this equation?

   a. ___ many   **b.** ___ one
   c. ___ none   **d.** ___ two

3. All the x's in Quadrant 2 are:

   a. ___ positive   **b.** ___ negative
   c. ___ positive and negative   **d.** ___ the same as the y's

ANSWERS: 1. a 2. c 3. b

TIP

You can write each x and y as an ordered pair. Write the x first and then the y.

 Keys to Understanding

Ordered Pairs

An **ordered pair** shows a special connection between an *x* and a *y*.
You can show that connection in a table. You can show it on a graph, too.

x	y
2	−5
0	−1
−2	3

ordered pair

(2, −5)
(0, −1)
(−2, 3)

To find ordered pairs:

• Find a number on the *x*-axis.
• Go up until you touch the line of the equation.
• Go across to the number on the *y*-axis.
• That *x* and that *y* will be an ordered pair.

Practice Problem: Complete the table for $y = -2x - 1$

x	y	Quadrant	Ordered Pair
2	−5	4	(2, −5)
0	−1	*y*-axis	(0, −1)
−2	3	2	(−2, 3)
1			
3			
−5			

Strategies for Test-Taking Success: Math © Thomson Heinle.
Photocopying this page is prohibited by law.

SEE PAGE 207 FOR ANSWERS.

Mean, Median, Mode

Pablo, Somsy, and Julia win a contest. Each winner can take the money from one box. Pablo chooses the box with the mean or average amount of money. Somsy chooses the box with the median amount. Julia chooses the box that is the mode. Who gets the most money?

 ## Keys to Understanding

The **mean** or **average** is the total number divided by each part.
The **median** is the middle number.
The **mode** is the number that occurs most often.
The **range** is the difference between the highest and lowest numbers.
The **total** is all the numbers added together.

ANSWERS: The mean or average is $16; the median is $15; and the mode is $7. Pablo gets the most money.

Word Problems: Use the data. Write the answer.

Five Houses

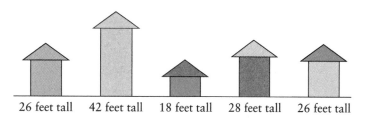

| 26 feet tall | 42 feet tall | 18 feet tall | 28 feet tall | 26 feet tall |

EXAMPLES

Mean or **Average** = total ÷ parts = 140 ÷ 5 = **28**
The mean of the house heights is **28** feet.

Median = 43 30 **26** 26 15
The middle of the heights from tallest to shortest is **26** feet.

Mode = two out of five houses are 26 feet tall
26 feet is the mode of the house heights.

Range = 42 − 18 = **24** feet

Total heights = 26 + 42 + 18 + 28 + 26 = **140** feet

There are five families in the five houses.
The first family has a mother, a father, and 5 children.
The second family has a mother, a father, a grandmother,
a grandfather, and 3 children.
The third family has a mother and 4 children.
The fourth family has a mother, a father, and 2 children.
The fifth house has 2 old brothers.

Practice Problems

1. What is the total number of people in all five houses?

2. What is the range of the family sizes?

3. Which family has the mean or average number of people?

4. Which family size is the mode?

5. Which family size is the median?

SEE PAGE 207 FOR ANSWERS.

Now, use your probability and data analysis skills to take a
Review Test.

CHAPTER 5: REVIEW TEST

Mark your answers on the Answer Grid.

Use this paragraph and the table to answer questions 1 through 3.

Billy fishes in a lake. There are 100 fish in the lake. There are 20 big catfish, 50 fat bluefish, and 30 little yellow fish. He catches 10 fish. Complete the table and decide what he catches.

Total Fish in the Lake = 100	
Ratio of **catfish** to **total**	
Ratio of **bluefish** to **total**	
Ratio of **yellow fish** to **total**	

1 How many catfish does he catch?

A. 2

B. 10

C. 20

D. 100

2 How many bluefish does he catch?

A. 5

B. 10

C. 50

D. 100

3 How many yellow fish does he catch?

A. 2

B. 3

C. 30

D. 100

Use this paragraph to answer questions 4 through 6.

Seven friends exchange gifts. They write their names on slips of paper. They put the slips of paper in a bag. Each person picks one slip of paper from the bag.

4 What is the probability that Roseanne will pull out her own name?

A. 1/7

B. 6/7

C. 7/7

D. 7/6

5 What is the probability that Roseanne will pull out someone else's name?

A. 1/7

B. 6/7

C. 7/7

D. 7/6

6 Roseanne picks one slip of paper and keeps it. It is not Fred's name. Then Fred picks a slip of paper. What is the probability that he will pick his own name?

A. 1/7

B. 1/6

C. 2/7

D. 2/6

GO ON

Monica asks her classmates what kind of music they like. The graph below shows the results. **Use the graph to answer questions 7 through 9.**

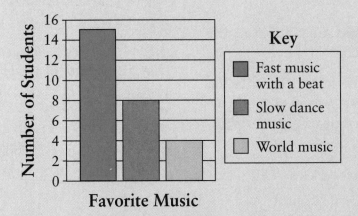

7 How many students like slow dance music?

A. 4

B. 8

C. 14

D. 22

8 How many more students like fast music with a beat than slow dance music?

A. 7

B. 8

C. 15

D. 23

9 How many students are in Monica's class?

A. 4

B. 8

C. 15

D. 27

GO ON

Use the circle graph to answer questions 10 through 12.

There are students from many countries in Bertrand's school. The circle graph shows the percent of students born in each part of the world.

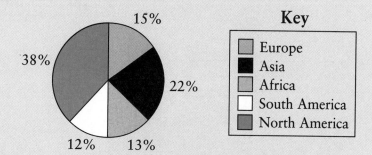

Key

- Europe
- Asia
- Africa
- South America
- North America

10 What percent of students were born in South America?

- A. 38%
- B. 22%
- C. 15%
- D. 12%

11 The number of students from Asia

- A. > the number of students from North America
- B. = the number of students from Europe
- C. ≤ the number of students from South America
- D. > the number of students from Africa

12 There are 1,200 students in Bertrand's school. How many students were born in North America?

- A. 38 students
- B. 46 students
- C. 456 students
- D. 600 students

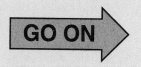

GO ON

Use the scatterplot and table to answer questions 13 through 15.

Nine boys on the baseball team have a contest. They want to see how far they can throw a baseball.

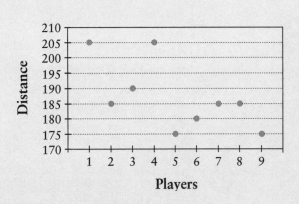

Player	Number
José	1
Juan	2
Len	3
Bill	4
Li	5
Andy	6
Seth	7
Jerry	8
Chris	9

13 Which players throw the baseball the farthest?

A. Chris and Andy

B. Juan and Li

C. José and Bill

D. Li and Chris

14 Which players throw the baseball 185 feet?

A. Juan, Seth, Jerry

B. José, Juan, Len

C. Seth, Jerry, Chris

D. Li, Andy, Chris

15 What is the shortest distance a player throws the ball?

A. 170

B. 175

C. 180

D. 185

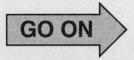

GO ON

Use the line graph to answer questions 16 through 19.

Sandy works at a music store. She gets four raises in the first six months.

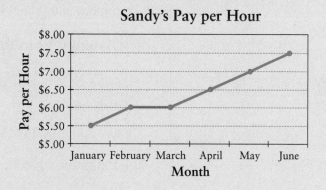

Sandy's Pay per Hour

16 What is Sandy's pay rate in January?

   A. $5.00 per hour

   B. $5.50 per hour

   C. $6.00 per hour

   D. $6.50 per hour

17 In which two months is Sandy's pay rate the same?

   A. January, February

   B. February, March

   C. March, April

   D. April, May

18 In which month does Sandy make the most money?

   A. March

   B. April

   C. May

   D. June

19 Look at the pattern of Sandy's raises. Estimate her pay per hour in July.

   A. $6.00

   B. $6.50

   C. $7.00

   D. $8.00

Use this graph to answer questions 20 and 21.

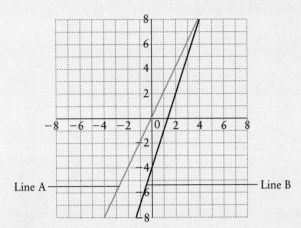

Line A ——— ——— Line B

20 Which line shows the equation:
$y = 2x$?

A. Line A

B. Line B

C. Lines A and B

D. No line

21 Which line shows the equation:
$y = 3x - 4$?

A. Line A

B. Line B

C. Lines A and B

D. No line

Use the table to answer questions 22 through 24.

Read the chart of driving distances between Philadelphia and other cities.

Distance from Philadelphia to:	
New York City	105 miles
Boston	320 miles
Washington, D.C.	130 miles
Baltimore	105 miles

22 What is the mean or average distance from Philadelphia to these four cities?

A. 130 miles

B. 150 mile

C. 165 miles

D. 320 miles

23 What distance is the mode?

A. 105 miles

B. 130 miles

C. 320 miles

D. 325 miles

24 What distance is the median?

A. 105 miles

B. 130 miles

C. 320 miles

D. 325 miles

STOP. THIS IS THE END OF THE REVIEW TEST.
SEE PAGE 208 FOR ANSWERS AND EXPLANATIONS.

Chapter

6

Geometry

Strategy 29 **Shapes**

Shapes are made with lines and angles.

straight line   curved line   angle

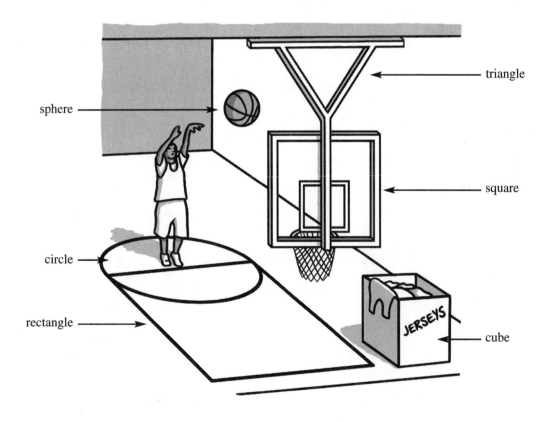

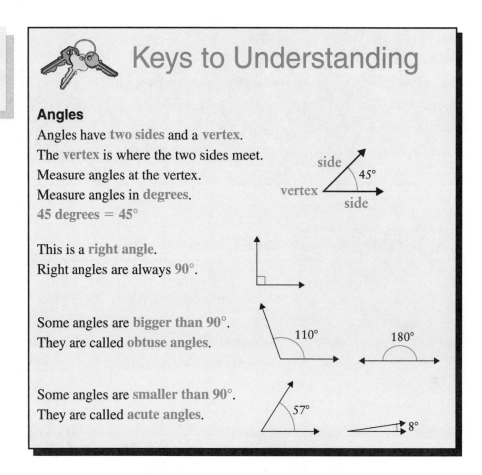

Keys to Understanding

Angles

Angles have **two sides** and a **vertex**.
The **vertex** is where the two sides meet.
Measure angles at the vertex.
Measure angles in **degrees**.
45 degrees = 45°

This is a **right angle**.
Right angles are always **90°**.

Some angles are **bigger than 90°**.
They are called **obtuse angles**.

Some angles are **smaller than 90°**.
They are called **acute angles**.

Sides or angles marked with the same number of lines are equal.

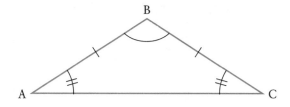

Angle A and Angle C have 2 lines. Angle A = Angle C

You can also use angle signs: ∠A = ∠C

Circles and Semicircles

TIP

Sometimes a test does not say: *circle, square,* or *rectangle.* It says: "Look at the **figure.**"

This is a **circle.**
A circle is made with a **curved, closed line.**

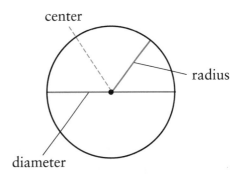

center

radius

diameter

A circle is **360 degrees.**

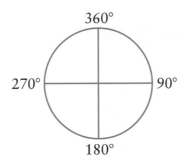

360°

270°   90°

180°

One-half of a circle is a semi-circle and is 180°.
A **diameter** is **180°.**
All **straight lines** are **180°.**

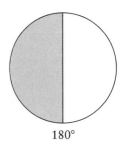

180°

Complete the sentences. Use a word from the box.

180	radius	diameter	✓360°

EXAMPLE

A circle is divided into degrees. A complete circle is <u>360°</u>.

1. The line called the _____ divides a circle in half.

2. A diameter divides the circle into _____ degrees.

3. A line from the center to the outside of the circle is called a

   _____ .

ANSWERS: 1. diameter 2. 180° 3. radius

Triangles

All **triangles** have 3 sides and 3 angles.
Together the 3 angles = **180°**.

A **right triangle** is a special triangle.
It has a right angle at the vertex.
A right angle has 2 sides.
The **third side** is called the **hypotenuse**.

Show a right angle vertex with a little **square**.

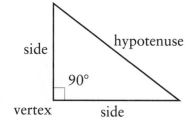

Circle the right triangles.

a. b. c. d. e. f.

ANSWERS: Triangles a, b, AND c are right triangles.

Figures with four sides are quadrilaterals. Rectangles and squares are quadrilaterals.

Rectangles have **4 sides** and **4 right angles**.

All angles are 90°.

Angles are named with a letter:
∠A ∠B ∠C ∠D
Sides are named with 2 letters:
    Side 1 is **AB**.
    Side 2 is **BD**.
    Side 3 is **DC**.
    Side 4 is **CA**.

Squares have **4 sides** and **4 right angles**.

All angles are 90°.

Angles are named with a letter:
∠P ∠Q ∠R ∠S
Sides are named with 2 letters:
    Side 1 is **PQ**.
    Side 2 is **QR**.
    Side 3 is **RS**.
    Side 4 is **SP**.

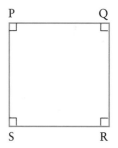

Opposite sides are **equal**.

Sides AB and CD are **equal**.
Sides AC and BD are **equal**.

All sides are **equal**.

Sides PQ, QR, RS, and SP are **equal**.

Write _S_ under the squares. Write _R_ under the rectangles.

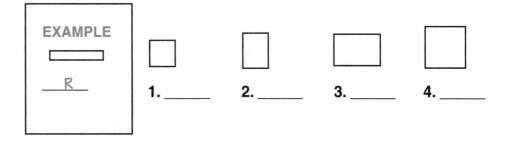

EXAMPLE

_R_

1. _____   2. _____   3. _____   4. _____

ANSWERS: 1. S 2. R 3. R 4. S

Circumference and Perimeter

The Distance Around

Mrs. Chin: The **perimeter** is the distance **around** a shape. The distance around a circle has a special name. It's called the **circumference** of a circle.
Give an example of times you measure a perimeter or a circumference.

Grace: My parents and I drove around Lake Michigan. They said that the perimeter of Lake Michigan is 1,300 miles.

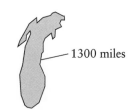
1300 miles

Ilya: I run around the park every evening. The distance all the way around the park is 2 1/3 miles. So the perimeter is 2 1/3 miles.

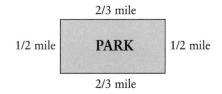
2/3 mile
1/2 mile PARK 1/2 mile
2/3 mile

Andrew: I need to buy a belt. I guess I need a Medium. The label says a Medium is 30 to 34 inches in circumference.

Medium: 30–34 inches

Isidro: I brought an apple for lunch. I want to know if I can put the whole apple in my mouth. Do I have to know the circumference of the apple and the perimeter of my mouth?

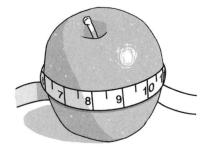

Circumference

The **circumference** is the distance around a circle.

A **ratio** compares two numbers. Write ratios like fractions.
The ratio of the **circumference** to the **diameter** of any circle = **pi**.

Sign for pi: π
Decimal for pi: **3.14** $\pi = 3.14$

You know the diameter. Use π to find the **circumference of a circle**.

Use the formula: $C = \pi d$ (Circumference = **3.14** × diameter)

$C = \pi d$

$C = 3.14 \times 7 = 21.98$

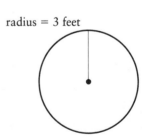

diameter = 7 inches

The circumference is 21.98 inches.

The **radius** goes from the center of the circle
to a point on its circumference.

radius = 3 feet

1 radius + 1 radius = 1 diameter

Circumference = **pi** × diameter
$C = \pi d$ or $C = \pi\,(2r)$
$\qquad C = 2\pi r$

The **radius** of the circle is **3 feet**. So the
diameter is **6 feet**.

$\begin{array}{ccc} C = 2\pi r & \quad\text{or}\quad & C = \pi d \\ C = 2 \times 3.14 \times 3 = 18.84 & & C = 3.14 \times 6 = 18.84 \end{array}$

The circumference is 18.84 feet.

Find the circumferences. Use a formula: $C = \pi d$ **or** $C = 2\pi r$

EXAMPLE

Diameter = 1.5 inches

$C = \pi d$

$C = 3.14 \times 1.5 = 4.71$

Circumference = 4.71 inches

---

1. Diameter = .5 inch

_____

2. Radius = 1.3 inches

_____

ANSWERS: 1. Circumference = 1.57 inches
2. Circumference = 8.164 inches

Perimeter

The **perimeter** is the distance around a shape.

Find the perimeters. Add all the sides together.

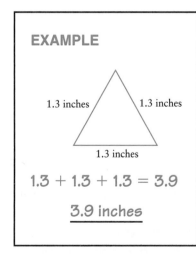

EXAMPLE

1.3 inches   1.3 inches

1.3 inches

$1.3 + 1.3 + 1.3 = 3.9$

3.9 inches

.75 inch
.75 inch   .75 inch
.75 inch

1. _____

2 inches
.5 inch   .5 inch
2 inches

2. _____

ANSWERS: 1. 3 inches 2. 5 inches

Strategies for Test-Taking Success: Math © Thomson Heinle. Photocopying this page is prohibited by law.

Similar Shapes

Similar shapes have **equal angles**.

Angle A = Angle D or $\angle A = \angle D$

Angle B = Angle C = Angle E = Angle F ($\angle B = \angle C = \angle E = \angle F$)

Similar shapes **may not have equal sides**.

Side AB ≠ Side DE

Side AC ≠ Side DF

Side BC ≠ Side EF

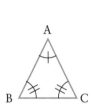
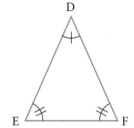

Ratios of Similar Shapes

A ratio compares the size of the similar sides of the two similar figures.

EXAMPLE A

Rectangle J and Rectangle K are similar.

Rectangle J: length = 30 inches, width = 6 inches
Rectangle K: length = 10 inches, width = y inches

Use ratios to find the width of Rectangle K.
All sides of similar figures will have the same ratio.
The ratio of the *similar* sides of these rectangles is 3:1.
Rectangle J is 3 times bigger than Rectangle K.

length of Rectangle J = 3 × length of Rectangle K

$$30 = 3 \times 10$$

width of Rectangle J = 3 × width of Rectangle K

$$\frac{6}{3} = \frac{3 \times y}{3}$$

$$2 = y$$

The width of Rectangle K is 2 inches.

Rectangle J

30 inches

6 inches

Rectangle K

10 inches

y inches

Triangle M and Triangle N are **similar**.

Triangle M

Triangle N

Triangle M: Side AB = 3 feet
Side BC = 4 feet
Side AC = 5 feet

Triangle N: DE = 1.5 feet
EF = 2 feet
DF = x

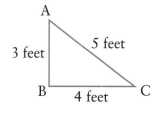

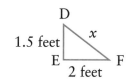

Use ratios to find DF.

The ratio of similar sides of these similar triangles is 2:1.
AC = 2 × DF
AC = 5 feet
$$\frac{5}{2} = \frac{2x}{2}$$
2.5 = x

DF = 2.5 feet

Find the width of side *z* in Rectangle G. Then find the perimeter of Rectangle G.

Step 1 Use the ratios of similar sides of similar rectangles to find the width of Rectangle G.

Rectangle F   Rectangle G

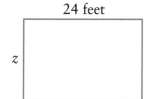

The width of *z* is _____ .

Step 2 Add all the sides to find the perimeter (length + length + width + width).

The perimeter of Rectangle G is _____ .

ANSWERS: The width of *z* is 16 feet. The perimeter of Rectangle G is 80 feet.

Area = **the number of squares** in a figure

The squares are always **1 unit long** and **1 unit wide**.

The units can be inches, feet, miles, or any other measurement.

The formula for area of a rectangle:

Area = **length × width** ($A = lw$)

EXAMPLE A

The width of Bernardo's bedroom is 10 feet. The length of Bernardo's bedroom is 11 feet. How many square feet are in Bernardo's bedroom?

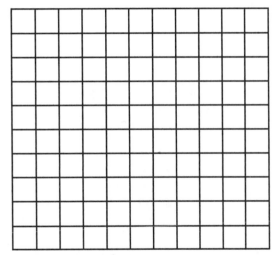

10 feet × 11 feet = 110 square feet (110 sq. ft.)

The area of Bernardo's bedroom is 110 square feet.

EXAMPLE B

The small gym at Carpenter Middle School has an area of 6,000 square feet. Its length is 75 feet. What is its width?

Use the formula: Area = length × width

$$A = lw$$
$$6,000 = 75w$$
$$\frac{6,000}{75} = \frac{75w}{75}$$
$$80 = w$$

The width of the gym is 80 feet.

EXAMPLE C

Blanca's mother invites the whole family to a birthday dinner. She puts three tables together. One table is a square with a side of 5 feet. One table is a square with a side of 3 feet. One table is a rectangle with a length of 6 feet and a width of 3 feet. What is the area of all the tables together?

Draw the problem.
Find the area of each table. Make a chart.   (feet = ft.)
Add the areas together.

Area = length × width ($A = lw$)

5 ft.

5 ft.   3 ft.   6 ft.

3 ft.   3 ft.

TABLES	AREA
First table	25 sq. ft.
Second table	9 sq. ft.
Third table	18 sq. ft.
Total Area	**52 sq. ft.**

Find the areas of the figures. Write the answers.

EXAMPLE

12 ft.

3 ft.

$A = lw$

$A = 12 \times 3$

$A = 36$ sq. ft.

4 in.

4 in.

2 mi.

5 mi.

1. _____   2. _____

ANSWERS: 1. 16 sq. in. 2. 10 sq. mi.

Area of Triangles

Right triangles are **1/2** the size of rectangles or squares.

The area of a right triangle is **1/2** the area of a square or rectangle.
The **base** of a triangle is the **bottom side**.
The **height** of the triangle is the **tall side**.

The formula for the **area** of a triangle is:
1/2 base × **height** or $A = 1/2\ bh$

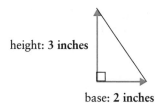

height: **3 inches**

base: **2 inches**

height: **14 ft.**

base: **10 ft.**

Area = 1/2 (3 × 2) = **3 square inches**   Area = 1/2 (14 × 10) = **70 sq. ft.**

Find the areas of the figures.

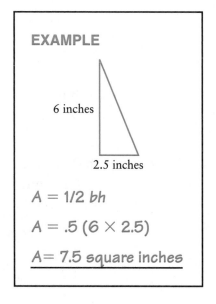

EXAMPLE

6 inches

2.5 inches

$A = 1/2\ bh$

$A = .5\ (6 × 2.5)$

$A = 7.5$ square inches

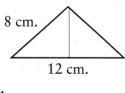

8 cm.

12 cm.

1. _____

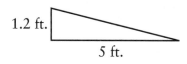

1.2 ft.

5 ft.

2. _____

ANSWERS: 1. 48 sq. cm. 2. 3 sq. ft.

Word Problems: Find the area. Write the answer.

EXAMPLE

The State of Colorado is almost a rectangle. It is 380 miles long (length) and 280 miles wide (width). What is the area of Colorado.

$A = l \times w$

$A = 380 \times 280$

$\underline{A = 106{,}400 \text{ square miles}}$

Practice Problems

1. Chloe is making a design. She has two triangles. The first triangle is half the size of the second triangle. The first triangle is 2 inches in height with a 3-inch base. What is the area of the second triangle?
   (HINT: Try using ratios of similar triangles. Use $A = 1/2\ bh$.)

2. What is the area of the figure below?

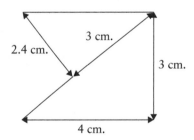

3. A hurricane hit a rectangular area of 24 square miles. It hit 8 miles of the shore (on the water). How far did it go inland from the water? (Try drawing a picture.)

4. A state park is 3 miles in length and 2 miles in width. The state wants to add some new land to the park. The new land is 1 mile in length and .75 of a mile in width. How big will the park be with the new land? (Try using a table.)

SEE PAGE 209 FOR ANSWERS.

The small number **2** in 5^2 is called an **exponent**. It tells you to multiply 5 by itself (5×5).

$5^2 = 5 \times 5 \qquad 14^2 = 14 \times 14 \qquad 100^2 = 100 \times 100$

These numbers are also called **squared numbers**.

The **formula** for the **area of a circle** is:

$$\text{Area} = \pi \times \textbf{radius} \times \textbf{radius}$$

Write the formula for the area of a circle:

$$A = \pi r^2$$

Circle A: radius = 1.5 inches

Area of Circle A

$A = \pi r^2$
$A = 3.14\,(1.5)^2$
$A = 3.14\,(1.5 \times 1.5)$
$A = 3.14\,(2.25)$
$A = 7.065$ square inches

A circle with a radius of 1.5 inches has an area of 7.065 square inches.

Find the areas of the figures.

EXAMPLE

Radius = .5 inch

$A = \pi r^2$

$A = 3.14\,(.5)(.5)$

$A = 3.14\,(.25)$

$A = .785$ square inches

Radius = 6 feet

1. _____

Radius = 2 miles

2. _____

ANSWERS: 1. 113.04 square feet 2. 12.56 square miles

Area of a Circle Inside a Square

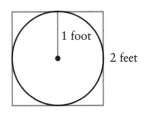

1 foot

2 feet

The **side** of the square = **2 feet**.
The **radius** of the circle = **1/2 × the side** of the square.
The **radius** of the circle = **1 foot**.
$A = \pi r^2$
$A = 3.14 \times 1 \times 1 = 3.14$
The area of the circle is 3.14 square feet.

Find the area of a circle inside a square. Write the answers.

1. Find the area of a circle inside a square with a side of 8 inches.

2. Find the area of a circle inside a square with a side of 5 centimeters.

ANSWERS 1. 50.24 square inches   2. 19.625 square centimeters

Word Problems: Find the area. Write the answer.

Practice Problems

1. A water sprinkler sprays water on a lawn. The arm of the water sprinkler is 3 feet long. What is the area of the circle of water? (HINT: The arm of the water sprinkler is the radius of the circle.)

2. Each side of a square is 5 inches. What is the area of the circle? (Hint: The radius of the circle = 1/2 of the side of the square.)

3. Shelly is cutting out cookies. She puts red frosting on top of the cookies. Each cookie has a radius of .5 inch. What is the area of the frosting on top of each cookie?

Strategies for Test-Taking Success: Math © Thomson Heinle. Photocopying this page is prohibited by law.

SEE PAGE 209 FOR ANSWERS.

Volume is how much a space holds.

The students in Mr. Banker's math class made boxes out of cardboard. The boxes are 1 foot in width, 1 foot in length, and 1 foot in height. Each box is a cube.

TIP

dimensions = size = measurements

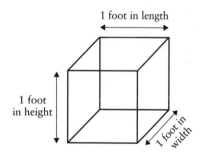

1 foot in length

1 foot in height

1 foot in width

The students put their boxes on top of each other in the closet.
The closet is 3 feet wide, 2 feet long, and 6 feet high. These are the **dimensions** of the closet.
The dimensions: $3' \times 2' \times 6' = 36$ **cubic** feet
The **volume** of the closet is **36 cubic** feet.
Each box is 1 cubic foot. The students can put 36 boxes in the closet.

The formula for volume of a cube is **length × width × height** or $V = lwh$.

Find the volumes of the figures.

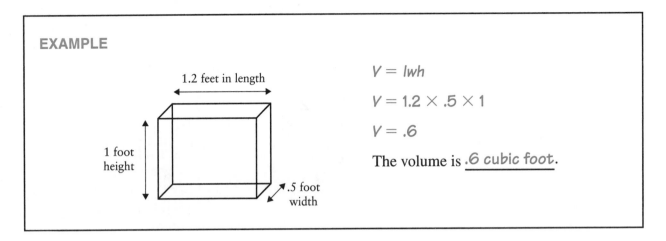

EXAMPLE

1.2 feet in length

1 foot height

.5 foot width

$V = lwh$

$V = 1.2 \times .5 \times 1$

$V = .6$

The volume is .6 cubic foot.

Box A

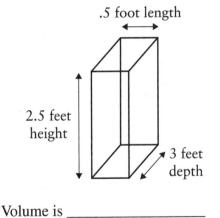

.5 foot length

2.5 feet height

3 feet depth

Volume is _____

Box B

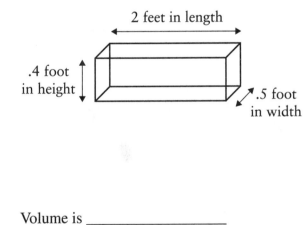

2 feet in length

.4 foot in height

.5 foot in width

Volume is _____

ANSWERS: Box A is 3.75 cubic feet. Box B is .4 cubic foot.

Word Problems: Find the volume.

EXAMPLE

There are two pieces of cake left. Pat wants the bigger piece. One piece of cake is 1 inch high, 2 inches wide, and 3 inches long. Pat figures that the volume is 6 cubic inches. The second piece of cake is 2 inches high, 2 inches wide, and 2 inches long. What is the volume of the second piece of cake?

$$V = lwh$$

$$V = 2 \times 2 \times 2 = 8 \text{ cubic inches}$$

Practice Problems

1. A bulldozer digs a hole for a basement. The basement is 40 feet long, 22 feet wide, and 8 feet deep. How many cubic feet of dirt does the bulldozer remove?

2. A box is 15 inches long, 8 inches wide, and 2 inches tall. The volume of the box is 240 cubic inches. Another box is also 15 inches long and 8 inches wide, but it is twice as tall. How does the volume of the second box compare to the volume of the first box? (HINT: Read the sentences. Find the volume of each box. How much bigger is the second box?)

Which answer is correct?

a. The volume of the second box is twice the volume of the first box.

b. The volume of the second box is the same as the volume of the first box.

c. The volume of the second box is 4 times the volume of the first box.

d. The volume of the second box is 1/2 times the volume of the first box.

SEE PAGE 209 FOR ANSWERS.

Pythagorean Theorem

Souk, Bethany, and AnnMarie wait for friends after school.

Souk says, "I can do some math magic. Look at the board. I'll tell you how long the diagonal is if you tell me how long the other two sides are."

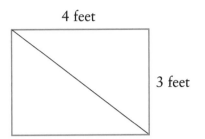

Bethany says, "Let's see you do it."

AnnMarie measures the two sides of the blackboard. They are 4 feet in length and 3 feet in width.

Souk thinks a minute. "The diagonal is 5 feet," he says.

How does Souk know?

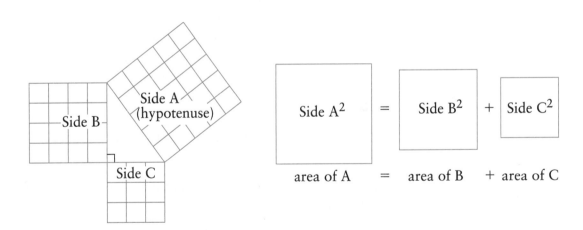

Another way to say this is: $A^2 = B^2 + C^2$

Side A × Side A = Side B × Side B + Side C × Side C

This is the **Pythagorean Theorem**.

The Pythagorean Theorem uses square numbers.
Make square numbers like A^2, B^2, and C^2 by multiplying a number by itself.
The number is the square root. The answer is the square.

square root square   square root square   square root square

$4 \times 4 = 16$ $3 \times 3 = 9$ $10 \times 10 = 100$

Write a square: $3^2 = 9$ Write a square root: $\sqrt{9} = 3$

EXAMPLE A

A lake is 6 miles in width and 8 miles in length. A man rows his boat from one corner of the lake to the other. How far does he row?

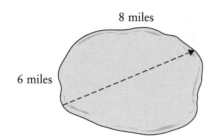

8 miles

6 miles

Use the Pythagorean Theorem.

$A^2 = B^2 + C^2$
$A^2 = 6^2 + 8^2$
$A^2 = 36 + 64$
$A^2 = 100$
$\sqrt{A^2} 5 \sqrt{100}$
$A = 10$

He rows 10 miles across.

EXAMPLE B

Caroline wants to copy a design from a display. She knows that the hypotenuses of the triangles are 15 inches. She knows that the shortest sides are 9 inches. How long are the other sides?

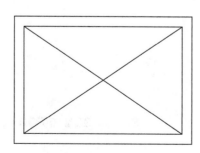

$A^2 = B^2 + C^2$
$15^2 = 9^2 + C^2$
$\mathbf{225} = 81 + C^2$
$225 - 81 = 81 - 81 + C^2$
$144 = C^2$
$\sqrt{144} = \sqrt{C^2}$
$12 = C$

The other sides are 12 inches.

Word Problems: Use the Pythagorean Theorem.

Practice Problems

1. Eddy cuts across the park to go to school. How much farther is it to walk around the park?

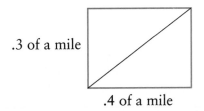

.3 of a mile

.4 of a mile

2. Armando throws a paper airplane out the window. The window is 5 feet from the ground. The plane lands 12 feet from the building. How far does the airplane fly?

3. Mr. Greylock drives across the bridge to go to work. The bridge is .5 mile long. One day the bridge is closed. He has to drive on Green Road and then on Woods Road. Look at the map. How far does he have to drive?

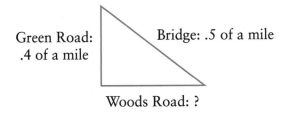

Green Road: .4 of a mile

Bridge: .5 of a mile

Woods Road: ?

SEE PAGE 210 FOR ANSWERS.

Rotation, Reflection, and Translation

Shapes can move on the coordinate grid.

Shapes can turn around or rotate. This is called **rotation**.

Vertex A is rotated from point (1,4) to point (3,4).

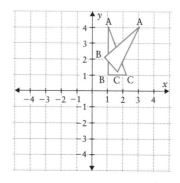

Shapes can flip over. This is called **reflection**.

The triangle is reflected over the y-axis.

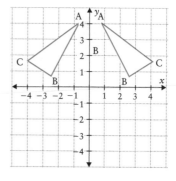

Shapes can slide. This is called **translation**.

The triangle is translated across the y-axis.

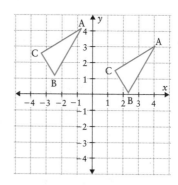

Practice: Label the pictures. Write *reflection, rotation,* or *translation.*

Picture 1

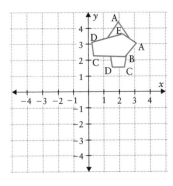

This figure makes a

_____.

Picture 2

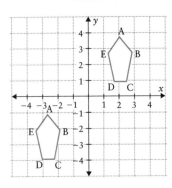

This figure makes a

_____.

Picture 3

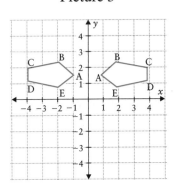

This figure makes a

_____.

ANSWERS: 1. rotation 2. translation 3. reflection

Now use your geometry skills to take a Review Test.

CHAPTER 6: REVIEW TEST

Mark your answers on the Answer Grid.

Use this list to complete questions 1 through 4.

circle

circumference

diameter

radius

rectangle

right angle

side

square

triangle

vertex

90

180

360

1 **Name the figures below.**

rectangle   A _____   B _____   C _____

2 **Label the parts of the angle.**

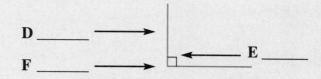

D _____

F _____

E _____

3 **Label the parts of the circle.**

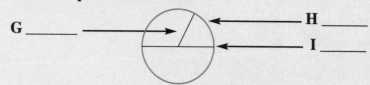

G _____

H _____

I _____

4 **Write the correct number of degrees in the space.**

A   All circles are _____ degrees.

B   All triangles are _____ degrees.

C   Each angle of a rectangle is _____ degrees.

5 **What is the perimeter of the triangle below?**

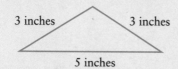

A   7.5 square inches

B   11 inches

C   13 inches

D   45 inches

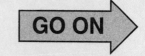

6 What is the circumference of the circle below?

Radius = 3 centimeters

A 9.42 centimeters

B 12 centimeters

C 18.84 centimeters

D 28.26 centimeters

7 Andros helps his parents fix their house. He needs to cut strips of wood to go around a window. The window is 3 feet wide and 4 feet high. How much wood does he need to cut?

A 7 feet

B 10 square feet

C 12 feet

D 14 feet

8 The parking lot at school is 80 feet wide and 90 feet long. The principal says that they need space for about 120 cars or 7,000 square feet. What is the area of the parking lot?

A 170 square feet

B 7,000 square feet

C 7,200 square feet

D 12,000 square feet

9 Which triangles are similar?

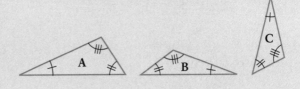

A Triangles A and B

B Triangles A and C

C Triangles A, B, and C

D None

10 What is the area of the triangle below?

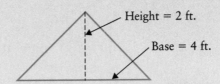

Height = 2 ft.

Base = 4 ft.

A 6 ft.

B 4 sq. ft.

C 8 sq. ft.

D 12 ft.

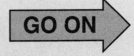

GO ON

Strategies for Test-Taking Success: Math © Thomson Heinle. Photocopying this page is prohibited by law.

11 **What is the area of the rectangle below?**

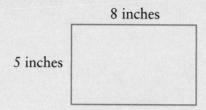

8 inches

5 inches

A 13 inches

B 26 inches

C 26 square inches

D 40 square inches

12 **What is the area of the figure below?**

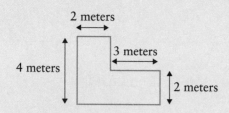

2 meters

3 meters

4 meters

2 meters

A 4 square meters

B 10 square meters

C 14 square meters

D 24 square meters

13 **What is the area of the circle below?**

Radius = 4 centimeters

A 12.56 square centimeters

B 16 centimeters

C 16 square centimeters

D 50.24 square centimeters

14 **What is the volume of this cube?**

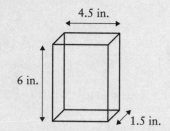

4.5 in.

6 in.

1.5 in.

A 12 inches

B 27 square inches

C 27 cubic inches

D 40.5 cubic inches

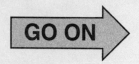

GO ON

15 There is a slide on the playground at the park. The ladder to the top of the slide is 8 feet tall. The distance from the bottom of the slide to the ladder is 15 feet. How long is the slide?

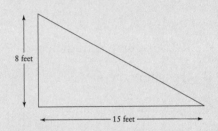

A 7 feet

B 17 feet

C 20 feet

D 23 feet

16 The figure on the coordinate axis below is an example of:

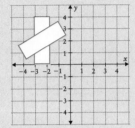

A rotation

B reflection

C translation

D hypotenuse

---

17 Rectangles 1 and 2 are similar figures. How long are sides EG and FH?

Rectangle 1   Rectangle 2

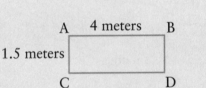 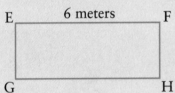

A 1.5 meters

B 2.25 meters

C 6 meters

D 7.5 meters

STOP. THIS IS THE END OF THE REVIEW TEST.
SEE PAGE 211 FOR ANSWERS AND EXPLANATIONS.

Strategies for Test-Taking Success: Math © Thomson Heinle.
Photocopying this page is prohibited by law.

Chapter 7 Put It All Together

Taking the Test

To do your best on a math test: **read**, **think**, and **organize**.

In this lesson, you will learn how to be a good math test-taker.
You will learn how to solve problems on a math test successfully.
You will also take two practice math tests.

Read

Read each problem carefully. Say the problem in your own words.

Think

Ask yourself: *What is this problem asking for? What do I need to do?*

Some problems ask you to work with numbers.

To put numbers together: Add

> It rained 7 days in June. It rained 4 days in July and 5 days in
> August. How much did it rain all summer?
>
> Put all the days together: $7 + 4 + 5 = 16$ days

To put groups of number together: Multiply

> A good rain lasts about 3 hours. It rained 16 days this summer.
> How many hours did it rain?
>
> Put 3-hour groups together: $16 \times 3 = 48$

To find the difference between numbers: Subtract

A day is 24 hours long. It rains for 3 hours. How many hours is it dry?

Take the wet hours away from all the hours: $24 - 3 = 21$

To take groups apart: Divide

It rains a total of 27 hours in May. There is only one rainstorm a day. Each rain lasts for 3 hours. How many days does it rain in May?

Take apart 3-hour groups of rain from the total hours:
$27 \div 3 = 9$

Some problems ask about math definitions.

Which triangles are similar?

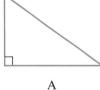

A   B   C

Definition: Similar triangles have **equal angles**. Triangles A and B are right triangles. They are similar.

Some problems ask for formulas.

What is the area of this rectangle?

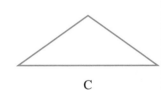

3 inches

6 inches

Use the formula: Area $=$ length $\times$ width ($A = lw$)
$6 \times 3 = 18$ square inches

Organize

Review the problem-solving strategies from Strategy 23 in Chapter 4 on page 95.

Easy problems: Do all the easy problems first. If a problem is too hard, go on to the next problem. When you finish all the easy problems, try the hard problems again.

- Make an estimate. Then do the problem.

- Write carefully and neatly. Then you can look again and understand what you did.

- Check your answer. Ask yourself: *Does this answer make sense? Is it close to my estimate? Does it match an answer on the test?*

- Check your math again. Mark your answer carefully on the answer sheet.

Hard problems: Sometimes a problem is hard to understand. Stay calm and **organize**. Go back and do hard problems *after* you finish all the easy ones.

- Read the problem again carefully. Look at the information in charts or diagrams.

- Ask yourself: *What do I need to know to find the right answer?*

- Try to remember a problem you did before that looks like this problem.

- Use problem-solving strategies. Sometimes you need one strategy. Sometimes you need more than one.

Sherry takes three tests. She gets 89 on the first test, 84 on the second test, and 95 on the third test. What is her average score?

Make a chart of what **you know** and what **you need to know**.

I know	I need to know
scores on tests: 89, 85, 96 **Average** means all the scores divided by the number of tests. **I need to do:** Step 1. Add the scores Step 2. Divide by 3	the average score $89 + 85 + 96 = 270$ $270 \div 3 = 90$

Make a guess: Sometimes you just can't figure out what to do. Read the question again. Then make a guess. Try to eliminate answers that don't make sense. Cross out answers you think are wrong. If you can cross out even one answer you improve your chances of getting the question right.

Out of time: Sometimes the test ends before you finish all the problems. Don't leave any blanks on your answer sheet. **Always make a guess.**

To get the best possible score: pick one letter. Mark **all your blank answers with the same letter**. You will have a better chance of getting some right.

Jan and Nan don't finish the last seven problems. So they guess. Here are parts of their answer grids. The answers in blue are correct.

Jan's answer

44. Ⓐ Ⓑ Ⓒ Ⓓ
45. Ⓐ Ⓑ Ⓒ Ⓓ
46. Ⓐ Ⓑ Ⓒ Ⓓ
47. Ⓐ Ⓑ Ⓒ Ⓓ
48. Ⓐ Ⓑ Ⓒ Ⓓ
49. Ⓐ Ⓑ Ⓒ Ⓓ
50. Ⓐ Ⓑ Ⓒ Ⓓ

Nan's answer

44. Ⓐ Ⓑ Ⓒ Ⓓ
45. Ⓐ Ⓑ Ⓒ Ⓓ
46. Ⓐ Ⓑ Ⓒ Ⓓ
47. Ⓐ Ⓑ Ⓒ Ⓓ
48. Ⓐ Ⓑ Ⓒ Ⓓ
49. Ⓐ Ⓑ Ⓒ Ⓓ
50. Ⓐ Ⓑ Ⓒ Ⓓ

Jan picks different letters for each answer. She gets one answer right. Nan uses the same letter for all her answers. She gets two answers right.

Using one letter for all blank answers can give you a better score.

Now, put your test-taking skills together to take
Cumulative Practice Test 1 and Cumulative Practice Test 2.

CUMULATIVE PRACTICE TEST 1

There are 45 math problems on this test. Mark your answers on the Answer Grid.

1 Shaleen loves shoes. She has 1 old pair of gym shoes and 1 new pair. She has 3 pairs of everyday shoes. She has 4 pairs of sandals and 1 pair of new, bright red heels. How many pairs of shoes does she have altogether?

A   4 pairs

B   7 pairs

C   10 pairs

D   15 pairs

2 There are 15 girls on the swim team. Each girl gets 4 tickets to the awards banquet. How many tickets does the team give out?

A   4 tickets

B   11 tickets

C   19 tickets

D   60 tickets

3 There are 1,440 minutes in a 24-hour day. Greg sleeps 480 minutes. How many minutes does he stay awake?

A   60 minutes

B   960 minutes

C   1,040 minutes

D   1,920 minutes

4 Ablavi has 1,248 pennies in a jar. Her sister gives her 567 pennies. Now how many pennies does she have?

A   681 pennies

B   1,705 pennies

C   1,815 pennies

D   707,616 pennies

5 Graduation is in the school gym. Students set up the chairs. They have 500 chairs. They put 20 chairs in each row. How many rows do they make?

A   25 rows

B   50 rows

C   480 rows

D   500 rows

6 In two weeks, Luan wants to walk 20 miles for charity. She practices every day. On Monday, she walks 2 miles. On Tuesday, she walks 4 miles. On Wednesday, she walks 6 miles. If she continues to increase her distance at this rate, how many miles does Luan walk on the tenth day?

A   8 miles

B   12 miles

C   20 miles

D   60 miles

7 Sam reads a recipe. He measures 3/4 of a cup of raisins. He looks at the recipe again. He has too many raisins. He pours out 1/4 of a cup of raisins. How many raisins does he have?

A   1 cup of raisins

B   1/2 cup of raisins

C   3/4 cup of raisins

D   2 cups of raisins

8 Frank cuts 5 pieces of wood. Each piece is 1/3 of a foot long. How many total feet of wood does he cut?

A   1/3 of a foot of wood

B   1 2/3 feet of wood

C   4 2/3 feet of wood

D   5 feet of wood

9 Abebe listens to two songs on his CD player. The first song lasts 2 1/2 minutes. The second song lasts 3 1/2 minutes. How long does he listen to music?

A   2 1/2 minutes

B   5 minutes

C   5 1/2 minutes

D   6 minutes

10 Betty stretches for a quarter of an hour. She runs for half an hour. How much does she exercise altogether?

A   1/4 of an hour

B   3/4 of an hour

C   1 hour

D   1 1/2 hours

11 The teacher tells everyone to make lines on a piece of paper. The paper is 8 1/2 inches long. Each line is 1/4 of an inch long. How many lines does each student need to draw?

A   8 1/2 lines

B   8 3/4 lines

C   34 lines

D   36 lines

GO ON

12 About 40% of Americans own dogs and 35% own cats. A small town has 2,000 people. No one owns more than one animal. How many dogs and cats are in the town?

A 75 dogs and cats

B 700 dogs and cats

C 800 dogs and cats

D 1,500 dogs and cats

Use this table to answer questions 13 through 15.

Everyone in Sergei's grade votes on a favorite color. The results are in the table.

Color	Favorite Color of 120 Students
Blue	.40
Green	.15
Red	.10
Black	.05
Purple	.05

13 How many students pick blue as their favorite color?

A 40 students

B 48 students

C 60 students

D 80 students

14 How many more students like blue than the next four colors altogether? Write the answer in decimals.

A .5 of the students

B .05 of the students

C .20 of the students

D .25 of the students

15 How many students have a favorite color that is not on the table? Write the answer in decimals.

A .25 of the students

B .35 of the students

C .40 of the students

D .60 of the students

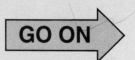
GO ON

16 Water covers between 70% and 75% of the Earth. How much of the Earth is dry land?

A Between 5% and 10% of the Earth is dry land.

B Between 25% and 30% of the Earth is dry land.

C Between 40% and 45% of the Earth is dry land.

D About 145% of the Earth is dry land.

17 The test has 84 questions. Zoë gets 63 questions right. What percent of her questions are right?

A 37% of the questions are correct.

B 16% of the questions are correct.

C 66% of the questions are correct.

D 75% of the questions are correct.

18 80% or 448 of the high school seniors plan to go to college. How many seniors are there?

A 368 seniors

B 479 seniors

C 528 seniors

D 560 seniors

DEXTER'S BANK BALANCE

Date	Amount
May 31	$89.00
June 5	− $5.00
June 12	+$20.00
June 25	−$10.00
July 3	−$30.00
July 15	+$50.00

19 How much money does Dexter have in the bank after he puts in $50.00 on July 15?

A $50.00

B $75.00

C $114.00

D $139.00

20 It is $-5°$ F in Chicago. It is 8 times colder in Billings, Montana. How cold is it in Billings?

A $-40°$ F

B $3°$ F

C $13°$ F

D $40°$ F

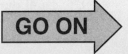

GO ON

21 The temperature is $-16°$. It increases by $3°$. What is the temperature now?

   A $-19°$

   B $-13°$

   C $-3°$

   D $16°$

22 Paul is trying to lose weight. He weighs 150 pounds now. He loses 2 pounds every week but then gains a pound back on the weekend. How much does he weigh in 5 weeks?

   A   155 pounds

   B   145 pounds

   C   140 pounds

   D   135 pounds

23 Sales tax is 7%. That means we pay .07 more for everything we buy. We can write this as an equation: $x + .07x = \text{cost}$. Use the equation to figure the cost for the items below:

        blue jeans: $20.00
        gym shoes: $75.00

   A   blue jeans: $20.07, gym shoes: $75.07

   B   blue jeans: $20.27, gym shoes: $75.77

   C   blue jeans: $21.40, gym shoes: $80.25

   D   blue jeans: $27.00, gym shoes: $82.00

24 Paniotes sells candy to raise money for the school basketball team. He makes $2.50 for each box of candy he sells. He makes a $.50 bonus for every box he sells over 30 boxes. What formula shows how much money he can make?

   A $\$2.50\,(30 + x)$

   B $\$2.50\,(x + .50)$

   C $\$2.50\,(30) + x$

   D $\$2.50x + .50\,(x - 30)$

GO ON

25 Mrs. Wilson gives candy to the girls at a sleepover. She has a bag with 50 small candy bars. Which equation shows how many candy bars each girl can have?

A $50 \div x =$ number of candy bars

B $50 + x =$ number of candy bars

C $50 - x =$ number of candy bars

D $50x =$ number of candy bars

26 In Mr. McGregor's class, a test grade of B is $>80\%$ and $\leq 90\%$. Match this inequality to the numbers.

A $\{80, 81, \ldots, 89, 90\}$

B $\{81, 82, \ldots, 89, 90\}$

C $\{81, 82, \ldots, 88, 89\}$

D $\{80, 81, \ldots, 88, 89\}$

27 A medicine label says that children >6 years old can take the medicine. Ali is 6. Gwen is 7. Charlie is 5. Mary is 12. Who can take the medicine?

A Ali, Gwen, Charlie, and Mary

B Ali, Gwen, and Mary

C Gwen and Mary

D Only Mary

28 One out of two 13-year-old girls is 5 feet 3 inches tall or taller. Which numbers below show this ratio?

A 1:2

B 1×2

C $1 + 2$

D 2 out of 1

29 There is a jar of marbles on Mr. Wendell's desk. It has 25 red marbles, 16 blue marbles, and 32 green marbles. What is the probability of picking out a red marble?

A 1 out of 25

B 1 out of 73

C 25 out of 73

D 25 out of 48

GO ON

Use these graphs to answer questions 30 and 31.

Ages of Boys and Girls with Allergies

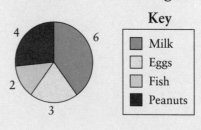

15 Children with Allergies

160 children are Dr. Lee's patients. Fifteen have food allergies. One chart shows how many boys and how many girls in each age group have allergies. The other chart shows different kinds of food allergies.

30 **What group by age and sex has the most allergies?**

A   Boys: ages 0 to 5

B   Girls: ages 5 to 10

C   Boys: ages 10 to 15

D   Girls: ages 10 to 15

31 **What percent of children is allergic to peanuts?**

A   2.5%

B   10%

C   40%

D   156%

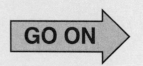

Jean-Pierre compares cars for a school project. He compares a car's weight and how many miles it goes on a gallon of gas. He puts his results in a graph.

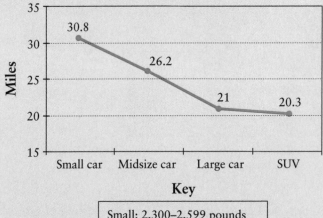

Miles on a Gallon of Gas

Key

Small: 2,300–2,599 pounds
Midsize: 2,600–2,999 pounds
Large: 3,001–3,499 pounds
SUV: over 3,500 pounds

32   **What does the graph show?**

A   All heavier cars use less gas than lighter cars.

B   The weight of a car affects how many miles the car can go on a gallon of gas.

C   Every small car goes 30.8 miles on a gallon of gas.

D   A midsize car goes 4.6 miles more for each gallon of gas than a small car.

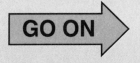

Julie has friends from all over the world. She and her friends use this graph to compare the average high temperatures in their home countries.

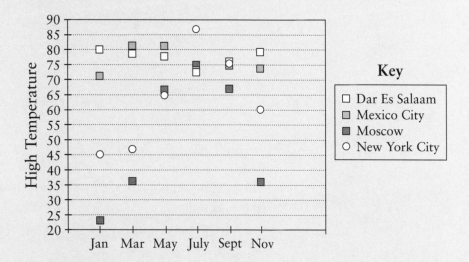

33 **Which month shows the biggest range of high temperatures for all the cities?**

A January

B March

C July

D November

$$y = 4x - 6$$

x	y
0	−6
1	−2
2	2
3	6

34 What is the ordered pair containing $x = 4$ in this equation of a line?

$$y = 4x - 6$$

A (4, 8)

B (4, −8)

C (4, 10)

D (10, 4)

GO ON

Use this table to answer questions 35 through 37.

This is a table of Afrim's test scores in science.

SCIENCE TEST SCORES

Date	Score
Sept. 20	82
Oct. 4	80
Oct. 18	83
Oct. 20	80
Nov. 1	94
Nov. 10	97
Nov. 20	100

35 What is the mode for these scores?

A 80

B 83

C 88

D 100

36 What is the mean for these scores?

A 80

B 83

C 88

D 100

37 What is the median of the scores?

A 80

B 83

C 88

D 100

38 The diameter of a pizza is 12.5 inches. What is its circumference? Use the formula: $C=\pi d$

A 15.64 inches

B 39.25 inches

C 122.66 inches

D 490.63 inches

39 Which number is closest to the area of the pizza? Use the formula: $A=\pi r^2$

A 15.64 square inches

B 39.25 square inches

C 122.66 square inches

D 490.63 square inches

40 Charles plays baseball. He hits a home run. He runs around all four bases. The distance from one base to another is 90 feet. We want to know how far Charles runs. What do we need to find?

A area

B circumference

C perimeter

D radius

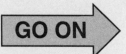

GO ON

41 Myriam wants to plant roses in a triangular garden. The sides are 8 feet and 15 feet. She needs to know how much space she has to plant. What is the area of the garden?

Use the formula: $A = 1/2\ bh$

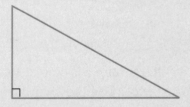

- A 60 square feet
- B 68 square feet
- C 120 square feet
- D 128 square feet

42 Myriam also wants to put stones around the garden. She has to find the perimeter to know how many stones to get. What is the perimeter of the garden?

- A 17 square feet
- B 40 feet
- C 120 feet
- D 289 feet

43 Harry loves ice cream. He buys a carton of chocolate ice cream at the store. He eats it all. The box is 8 inches long, 5 inches wide, and 4 inches high. How many cubic inches of ice cream does he eat? Use the formula: $V = lwh$

- A 17 cubic inches of ice cream
- B 32 cubic inches of ice cream
- C 40 cubic inches of ice cream
- D 160 cubic inches of ice cream

44 Pedro stands in the sun. From his head to the end of his shadow is 13 feet. From his feet to the end of his shadow is 12 feet. How tall is Pedro?

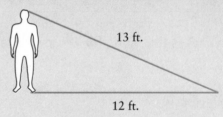

- A 6 feet
- B 5.5 feet
- C 5 feet
- D 4.5 feet

GO ON

45 Zahra looks at distances on a map. She uses what she knows about similar triangles to find the distance from Elgin to Carpenters Park. What is the distance?

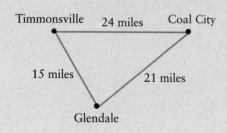

Timmonsville — 24 miles — Coal City

15 miles   21 miles

Glendale

Elgin — 16 miles — Greentown

14 miles

Carpenters Park

A 5 miles

B 8 miles

C 10 miles

D 15 miles

STOP. THIS IS THE END OF CUMULATIVE PRACTICE TEST 1. SEE PAGE 212 FOR ANSWERS AND EXPLANATIONS.

CUMULATIVE PRACTICE TEST 2

There are 45 math problems on this test. Mark your answers on the Answer Grid.

1 John takes the change out of his pocket. He has 25¢, 25¢, 10¢, 5¢, and 1¢. How much money does he have?

A 5¢

B 12¢

C 66¢

D 111¢

2 There are 365 days in a year. Jack doesn't work on the 104 weekend days. He also gets 10 days of vacation and 10 holidays. How many days a year does he have to work?

A 241 days

B 259 days

C 261 days

D 479 days

3 Mt. Whitney in California and Mt. Rainier in Washington are the two tallest mountains in the lower United States. Mt. Whitney is 4,418 feet tall. Mt. Rainier is 4,393 feet tall. How much taller is Mt. Whitney?

A 15 feet

B 25 feet

C 185 feet

D 9,811 feet

4 There are 1,000 seats in the school auditorium. Each row has 40 seats. How many rows are there?

A 25 rows

B 50 rows

C 480 rows

D 500 rows

5 Tom arranges oranges in rows at the grocery store. He puts 12 oranges in the first row, 10 oranges in the second row, and 8 oranges in the third row. He continues to make rows until the last row has 2 oranges. How many rows will he make altogether?

A 3 rows

B 6 rows

C 12 rows

D 30 rows

GO ON

6 Suzy was 5 feet and 1/4 inch tall in September. Now she is 5 feet and 3/4 inch tall. How much did she grow?

A 1/4 inch

B 1/2 inch

C 1 inch

D 4 inches

7 Sophie eats 1 1/2 ears of corn for dinner. Her brother, Rick, eats 2 ears of corn. Her other brother, Charlie, eats 2 1/2 ears of corn. Suzy's mother and father eat 1 ear each. How many ears of corn should Suzy's parents buy?

A 1 1/2 ears

B 3 1/2 ears

C 6 ears

D 8 ears

8 Gabriel reads 2/3 of his 54-page book for homework. How many pages does he read?

A 18 pages

B 36 pages

C 72 pages

D 81 pages

9 Alex needs one can of oil for the car. He has one can that is half full. He has another can that is one-third full. How much oil does he have in both cans?

A 2/3 of a can

B 5/6 of a can

C 1 can

D 1 1/6 cans

10 An ice cream cone holds 2/3 of a cup of ice cream. How many cones can you make from a 48-cup carton of ice cream?

A 32 cones

B 48 cones

C 72 cones

D 96 cones

11 About 55% of Americans vote in presidential elections. There are 12,000 people in Charlotte's town. How many people in Charlotte's town vote in the presidential election?

A 160 people

B 6,600 people

C 9,000 people

D 11,025 people

GO ON

Use this table to answer questions 12 through 14.

Some juices have a lot of real fruit juice. Some juices have a lot of sugar water. Fran reads some juice labels and makes a table.

Juice Name	Amount of Real Fruit Juice
Sun Orange Juice	.90
Sunday Orange Juice	.20
Autumn Apple Juice	.35
Sweet Grape Juice	.15
White Grape Juice	.80

12 How many juices are more than 1/2 real fruit juice?

A 2 of the juices

B 3 of the juices

C 4 of the juices

D 5 of the juices

13 How much more real fruit juice does Sun Orange Juice have than Sweet Grape Juice?

A .15 more real juice

B .135 more real juice

C .75 more real juice

D .90 more real juice

14 Autumn Apple Juice is .35 real juice and the rest is sugar water. How much is sugar water?

A .03 sugar water

B .35 sugar water

C .60 sugar water

D .65 sugar water

15 Mrs. Brown makes salad dressing. The recipe says to add 1 tablespoon of vinegar for every 2 tablespoons of oil. She uses 6 tablespoons of vinegar. How much oil should she add?

A 2 tablespoons of oil

B 6 tablespoons of oil

C 8 tablespoons of oil

D 12 tablespoons of oil

16 The sun shines on 12 of the 30 days in November. What percent of the time does the sun shine?

A 12% of the time

B 28% of the time

C 30% of the time

D 40% of the time

17 65% of the cars on the road are blue. Victor sees 40 cars pass his bus stop. How many are blue?

A 20 cars

B 25 cars

C 26 cars

D 40 cars

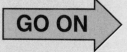
GO ON

18 All of the students in Mrs. Gross's class begin the year with 50 points. They can lose points or get more points. At the end of the year, everyone with 40 points or more gets a prize. How many points does Alison have?

Alison's Points (She starts the year with 50 points.)	
Talks in class	−5
Comes in late	−10
Has a perfect test	+10
Helps a friend study	+5
Talks in class	−5
Brings in all homework	+10

A −20 points

B +5 points

C +45 points

D +55 points

19 A submarine sinks 30 feet into the water. It does this 5 times. How deep is it now?

A 150 feet

B −25 feet

C −35 feet

D −150 feet

20 Stasek takes a piece of string 6 feet long and cuts it in thirds. Then he cuts each piece in thirds again. How many pieces does he have and how long are they?

A 3 pieces, 2 feet each

B 9 pieces, 2/3 of a foot each

C 18 pieces, 1/2 foot each

D 18 pieces, 2/3 of a foot each

21 Luis eats in a restaurant. He pays for his dinner and a 15% tip. His dinner is $23.60. What is his total cost?

> x = the cost of his dinner
> $.15x$ = the cost of his tip
> The total cost is $x + .15x$.

A $3.54

B $23.75

C $25.96

D $27.14

22 Many countries use Celsius to measure temperature. The United States uses Fahrenheit. If the temperature is 50° Fahrenheit, what is it in Celsius?

Use the formula:
Celsius = (Fahrenheit − 32) × 5/9

A −4.2° Celsius

B 10° Celsius

C 18° Celsius

D 45.5° Celsius

23 A 3-year-old boy is 3.5 feet tall. He is already at 55% of his adult height. What formula shows this?

A $.55h$

B $h + .55$

C $h + 5.5$

D $h \div .55$

24 Mr. Rodriquez has 50 sharp pencils ready for a test. The number of students is x. Which equation shows how many pencils he can give to each student?

A $50 \div x$ = number of pencils

B $50 + x$ = number of pencils

C $50 - x$ = number of pencils

D $50x$ = number pencils

25 The number of days in a month is between 28 and 31. We can write this inequality as: days in a month ≥ 28 and ≤ 31. Match this inequality to the numbers.

A $\{28, \ldots, 30\}$

B $\{28, \ldots, 31\}$

C $\{29, 30\}$

D $\{29, \ldots, 31\}$

26 The sign at the hospital says that children ≤ 12 cannot visit without a parent. Bridget is 12. Mary is 11 and Charles is 13. Alex is 9. Who can visit without a parent?

A   Bridget, Mary, Charles, and Alex

B   Bridget, Mary, and Charles

C   Bridget and Charles

D   Only Charles

27 Eight out of ten sports injuries happen in four sports: basketball, football, soccer, and baseball. Which numbers below show this ratio?

A 8×10

B   8:10

C $8 + 10$

D   10 out of 8

28 Derrick reaches in a box to get his prize at the school carnival. There are 200 whistles in the box, 100 puzzles, 50 sunglasses, and 25 toy racing cars. What is the probability that Derrick will pull out a car?

A   1 out of 8

B   1 out of 15

C   1 out of 25

D   25 out of 200

GO ON

Use these graphs to answer questions 29 and 30.

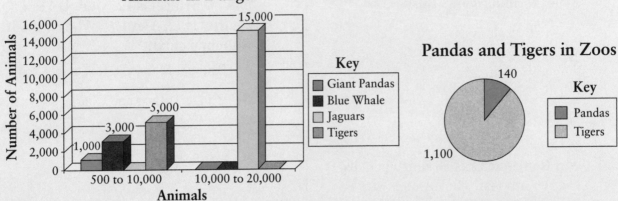

Giant pandas, blue whales, tigers, and jaguars are disappearing from the world. The first chart shows how many of these animals live outside zoos. The second chart shows how many pandas and tigers are living inside zoos.

29 **How many tigers are living outside zoos?**

A   1,000 tigers

B   3,000 tigers

C   5,000 tigers

D   15,000 tigers

30 **The ratio of tigers to pandas outside of zoos is 5:1. What is the ratio of tigers to pandas in zoos?**

A   about 8:1

B   about 10:2

C   about 1000:1

D   about 1000:2

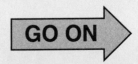

Raj records his swimming times for the 50-yard freestyle on a graph.

Time in Seconds for 50-Yard Freestyle

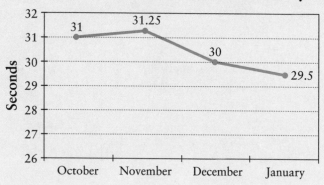

31 **What is Raj's fastest time?**

A   29.5 seconds

B   30 seconds

C   31 seconds

D   31.25 seconds

Countries have different speed limits. This chart shows the speed limits on the highway for some countries in Europe.

Speed Limits on the Open Road in km/hr

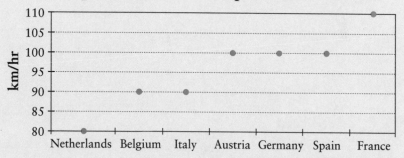

32 **What is the difference between the speed limits in the Netherlands and in France?**

A   25 km/hr

B   30 km/hr

C   35 km/hr

D   40 km/hr

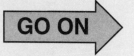

$$y = 3x - 5$$

x	y
0	-5
1	-2
2	1
3	4

33 What is the ordered pair containing $x = 4$ in this equation of a line?

$$y = 3x - 5$$

A $(4, -17)$

B $(4, 7)$

C $(4, 12)$

D $(4, 17)$

GO ON

Use this table to answer questions 34 through 36.

The table below shows the temperatures for Bismarck, North Dakota, for the first 15 days in January.

Temperatures: Bismarck, North Dakota

January 1	$-2°$	January 8	$12°$
January 2	$2°$	January 9	$4°$
January 3	$-10°$	January 10	$12°$
January 4	$-15°$	January 11	$-5°$
January 5	$-17°$	January 12	$0°$
January 6	$-5°$	January 13	$-5°$
January 7	$-5°$	January 14	$-10°$
		January 15	$-1°$

34 **What is the mean temperature?**

A -17

B -5

C -3

D 0

35 **What is the median temperature?**

A -17

B -5

C -3

D 0

36 **What is the mode for these temperatures?**

A -17

B -5

C -3

D 0

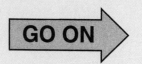
GO ON

37 Alesha gets a very large chocolate chip cookie as a birthday present. Its diameter is 15 inches. What is its circumference? Use the formula: $C\pi d$

A 18.4 inches

B 45 inches

C 47.1 inches

D 706.5 inches

38 Carol and her family want to make a circle for ice-skating in the backyard. They have space for a circle with a diameter of 20 feet. How much skating area will they have? Use the formula: $A=\pi r^2$

A 31.4 square feet

B 62.8 square feet

C 314 square feet

D 1,256 square feet

39 The Oldham family is moving into a new house. They have three bedrooms. Ann wants the biggest bedroom. The first bedroom is 10 feet long and 11 feet wide. The second bedroom is 9 feet long and 12 feet wide. The third bedroom is 10 feet long and 10 feet wide. Which bedroom is the biggest?

A The first bedroom is the biggest.

B The second bedroom is the biggest.

C The third bedroom is the biggest.

D They are all the same size.

40 Barbara and Hassim are painting a picture on a wall in the school. They need to know how much paint to get for a large red triangle. The triangle is 6 feet long and 8 feet wide. Use the formula: $A=1/2\ bh$

A 14 square feet

B 24 square feet

C 48 square feet

D 64 square feet

41 What is the area of the biggest circle that Harry can cut from a square piece of wood? Each side of the wood is 16 inches.

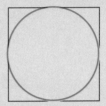

A 64 square inches

B 200.96 square inches

C 256 square inches

D 803.84 square inches

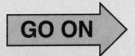

42 Anthony helps his father build a porch. First they fill the space under the porch with stones. The space is 12 feet wide, 8 feet long, and .5 feet high. How many cubic feet of stones do they have to buy? Use the formula: $V=lwh$

A   10 cubic feet of stones

B   25 cubic feet of stones

C   48 cubic feet of stones

D   480 cubic feet of stones

43 John builds a skateboard ramp. It is 3 feet high and 4 feet long. How long is the ramp?

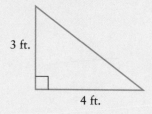

3 ft.

4 ft.

A   1 foot

B   5 feet

C   7 feet

D   12 feet

44 Bethany makes cookies for her class. She has two cookie sheets that are the same shape. She knows that one cookie sheet is 14 inches long and 8 inches wide. She knows the second cookie sheet is 21 inches long. How wide is it?

A   10 inches wide

B   11 inches wide

C   12 inches wide

D   13 inches wide

45 The figure on the coordinate grid is an example of what?

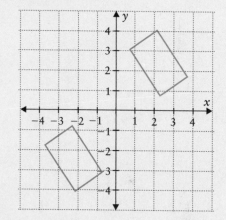

A   rotation

B   reflection

C   translation

D   dimension

STOP. THIS IS THE END OF CUMULATIVE PRACTICE TEST 2.
SEE PAGE 215 FOR ANSWERS AND EXPLANATIONS.

Sun	Mon	Tue	Wed	Thu	Fri	Sat
	1 *Today:* *Make a* *plan*	2 *5:00–6* *Study* *time* ✓	3 *5:00–6* *Study* *time* ✓	4 *5:00–6* *Study* *time* ✓	5 *5:00–6* *Study* *time* ✓	6 *5:00–6* *Study* *time* ✓
7	8 *5:00–6* *Study* *time* ✓	9 *5:00–6* *Study* *time* ✓	10 *Study for* *science* *test*	11 *5:00–6* *Study* *time* ✓	12 *5:00–6* *Study* *time* ✓	13 *5:00–6* *Study* *time* ✓
14	15 *5:00–6* *Study* *time* ✓	16 *5:00–6* *Study* *time* ✓	17 *5:00–6* *Study* *time* ✓	18 *5:00–6* *Study* *time* ✓	19 *Birthday* *party* *for Dad*	20 *5:00–6* *Study* *time* ✓
21	22 *5:00–6* *Study* *time* ✓	23 *5:00–6* *Study* *time* ✓	24 *5:00–6* *Study* *time* ✓	25 *5:00–6* *Study* *time* ✓	26 *5:00–6* *Study* *time* ✓	27 *School* *play*
28	29 *4:00–6* *Soccer*	30 *RELAX*	31 *TEST*			

You have studied the skills you need. You have practiced good test-taking strategies. You are ready for the test. Here are some ideas to get you through test week.

Relax. This is a tense week. Be sure to take time to relax and have some fun.

Be positive about your work. Focus on what you know and what you can do.

Get regular physical exercise. Don't forget to balance school work and exercise. Exercise helps your body be stronger. It also helps you sleep well so you can learn better.

Strategies for Test-Taking Success: Math © Thomson Heinle.
Photocopying this page is prohibited by law.

On the night before the test:

- **Prepare for the test day.** Organize the things you will need for the test. Here is a sample list:

  - sharpened pencils and erasers
  - a pen and paper
  - fruit or other healthy snacks for breaks
  - eyeglasses
  - watch
  - a sweater or sweatshirt (in case the room is cold)

- **Eat dinner.** Drink a glass of milk too. The calcium in milk relaxes you naturally.

- **Relax and don't study.** Cramming (studying at the last minute) doesn't help. It makes you worry.

- **Set the alarm.** You don't want to be late for school. Set it early enough to have time for breakfast. Get a good night's sleep.

On the morning of the test:

- **Eat breakfast.** You can't do your best without it!

At the test:

- **Focus on your work.** Don't waste time worrying about yourself or wondering how other people are doing. Don't worry about what you did before or what may happen in the future. Pay attention to *what you can do now*.

- **Ask questions.** If you don't understand the directions or if you aren't sure about what to do, ask the teacher.

- **Estimate before you work on a problem.** Estimating helps you to understand the whole problem before you start calculating the answer.

- **Answer the easy questions first.** Then go back and try the hard ones. Don't spend a lot of time on one question or you won't have enough time to finish the test.

- **Always make a guess.** Pick the best answer you can even if you have to guess between two choices. If you still have any blanks, pick one letter and mark any blanks left with that letter.

Good Luck!

Glossary

Angle the space between two connected lines, measured in degrees

Area measurement of surface *inside* a figure

Bar graph a graph with bars to compare individual items, with the height of each bar showing data

Calculate using the rules of mathematics to solve problems

Circle a geometric figure made of a continuous curved line with all points on the circle the same distance from its center

Circle graph a graph using a circle, with the circle symbol standing for the whole thing and the parts of the circle standing for the parts of the whole thing

Circumference the perimeter of (distance around) a circle

Coordinate grid an area divided into squares. Two lines separate the squares into four parts or quadrants. One line is the horizontal axis and one line is the vertical axis.

Cube a geometric figure that is the shape of a box

Data information, numbers, or quantities

Decimal point a point that separates a whole number from its decimals

Decimals parts of a hundred

Degrees measurement for the space in a shape (A circle has 360 degrees.)

Denominator the bottom number in a fraction (A denominator shows all the equal-sized parts of a whole.)

$$\frac{2}{3} = \text{denominator}$$

Diameter a line that goes from one point of a circle to its opposite side, through the center of the circle

Display a way to show information on a graph

Dividend the number that is divided into parts in a division problem

$$6 \div 3 \quad \text{or} \quad 3\overline{)6} \quad \text{6 is the \textbf{dividend}}$$

Divisor the number that divides another number into parts

$$6 \div 3 \quad \text{or} \quad 3\overline{)6} \quad \text{3 is the \textbf{divisor}}$$

Equals the same amount

$$2 + 5 = 7$$

Equation two mathematical expressions that are equal

$$2 + 5 = 4 + 3$$

Equivalent means equal: use equivalent to show different ways to write the same amount

$$3 = \text{three} = \triangle \ \triangle \ \triangle$$

Estimate use your understanding of numbers to guess the answer to a mathematical problem

Greater than bigger than

Height how tall something is

Horizontal a line that runs side to side

Inequalities comparing two amounts and deciding if they are equal or one is bigger than the other

Interval the space between two numbers

Less than smaller than

Line graph a graph where a line shows changes across time or distance

Line of best fit a line on a scatterplot that comes closest to all the points

Mean, average the sum of a group of numbers divided by the number of the whole group

Measurement a tool to figure size; the unit can be inches, centimeters, miles, or any other standard unit

Median the number in the middle of a group of numbers

Mixed numbers a whole number with a fraction

$$1\frac{5}{6}$$

Mode the number you see most often in a group of numbers

Multiplication adding groups

Negative numbers less than zero

Numerator the top number in a fraction; numerator shows the parts of one quantity

$$\frac{2}{3} = \text{numerator}$$

Operation addition, subtraction, multiplication, or division

Ordered pair two numbers that show a point on a graph, with the first number showing how far the point is horizontally from the center of the graph and the second number showing how far the point is vertically from the center of the graph

Pattern a repeated design of numbers or things

Percents describe parts of a whole; compare parts of 100 to parts of a whole

Perimeter the distance *around* a figure

Pi the circumference of a circle divided by its radius, pi (also written as π) equals 3.14

Positive numbers greater than zero

Probability a ratio that shows how possible it is that something will happen

$$1 \text{ time out of } 3 \text{ or } \frac{1}{3}$$

Product the answer to a multiplication problem
$$7 \times 8 = 56$$

Pythagorean Theorem $a^2 = b^2 + c^2$ where b and c are the sides of a right triangle and a is the hypotenuse

Quadrant the coordinate grid divided into four parts with each part a quadrant

Quotient the answer to a division problem

Radius a line from the center of a circle to any point on the circle; one half a diameter

Range the distance between the lowest and highest numbers

Ratio comparing two numbers

Rectangle a geometric figure with four sides and four 90-degree angles

Scatterplot a graph with many points. Each point is a symbol for a piece of data.

Semicircle half a circle

Similar shapes shapes that are not the same size but have the same angles and the same number of sides

Sphere a geometric object that is the shape of a ball

Square a geometric figure with four equal sides and four 90-degree angles

Square number the answer (product) of multiplying a number by itself
$$3 \times 3 = 9$$
Nine is a square number. You can draw a square number as a square.

Straight line a line that does not bend (A straight line has 180 degrees.)

Table a chart where you write data

Triangle a geometric figure with three sides

Variable a letter that stands for an unknown number in an equation
$$x + y = 24$$
x and y are variables in this equation.

Vertex two lines that make an angle join at the vertex

Vertical a line that makes a right angle with a horizontal line

x-axis the horizontal line on a graph

y-axis the vertical line on a graph

Glosario

Angle (Ángulo) Espacio entre dos líneas que se conectan, medido en grados.

Area (Área) Medida de la superficie *interior* de una figura.

Bar graph (Gráfico de barras) Gráfico con barras para comparar datos, donde la altura de cada barra equivale a una cantidad.

Calculate (Calcular) Usar las reglas de las matemáticas para solucionar problemas.

Circle (Círculo) Figura geométrica formada por una línea curva continua, donde todos los puntos del círculo se encuentran a la misma distancia de su centro.

Circle graph (Gráfico circular) Gráfico que usa un círculo; el círculo representa la totalidad de una cosa y las partes del círculo representan partes de esa totalidad.

Circumference (Circunferencia) Perímetro (distancia alrededor) de un círculo.

Coordinate grid (Plano coordenado) Área dividida en cuatro partes o cuadrantes por dos líneas que se cruzan. Una línea es el eje horizontal y la otra el eje vertical.

Cube (Cubo) Figura geométrica que tiene la forma de una caja.

Data (Datos) Información, números o cantidades.

Decimal point (Punto decimal) Punto que separa un número entero de sus decimales.

Decimals (Decimales) Partes de un ciento.

Degrees (Grados) Unidad de medida de ángulos o arcos (Un círculo tiene 360 grados).

Denominator (Denominador) El número que se encuentra en la parte inferior de una fracción (un denominador muestra todas las partes iguales de un todo).

$$\frac{2}{3} = \text{denominador}$$

Diameter (Diámetro) Línea recta que va de un punto de un círculo al lado opuesto, cruzando por el centro del círculo.

Display (Presentación) Forma de mostrar información en un gráfico.

Dividend (Dividendo) El número que se divide en partes en un problema de división:

$$6 \div 3 \text{ ó } 6\overline{)3} \quad \text{6 es el } \textbf{dividendo}$$

Divisor (Divisor) El número que divide a otro número en partes:

$$6 \div 3 \text{ ó } 6\overline{)3} \quad \text{3 es el } \textbf{divisor}$$

Equals (Igual a) La misma cantidad:

$$2 + 5 = 7$$

Equation (Ecuación) Dos expresiones matemáticas que son iguales:

$$2 + 5 = 4 + 3$$

Equivalent (Equivalente) Significa "igual a". El concepto de equivalente se usa para mostrar diferentes maneras de escribir la misma cantidad:

$$3 = \text{tres} = \triangle \ \triangle \ \triangle$$

Estimate (Estimar) Usar tu conocimiento de los números para deducir la respuesta de un problema matemático.

Greater than (Mayor que) Significa "más grande que".

Height (Altura) Qué tan alto es algo.

Horizontal (Horizontal) Una línea que va de lado a lado.

Inequalities (Desigualdades) Comparar dos cantidades y decidir si son iguales o si una es más grande que la otra.

Interval (Intervalo) El espacio entre dos números.

Less than (Menor que) "Más pequeño que".

Line graph (Gráfico lineal) Gráfico en el que una línea muestra cambios en **tiempo** o **distancia**.

Line of best fit (Línea que mejor encaja) Línea en un diagrama de dispersión que se acerca más a todos los puntos.

Mean, average (Media, promedio) La suma de una serie de cantidades dividida entre el número de cantidades.

Measurement (Medida) Herramienta para determinar tamaños: la unidad de medida puede ser pulgadas, centímetros, millas o cualquier otra unidad estándar.

Median (Valor medio) El número en la mitad de los extremos de un grupo de números.

Mixed numbers (Números mixtos) Un número entero con una fracción:

$$1\frac{5}{6}$$

Mode (Moda) El número que ves con más frecuencia en un grupo de números.

Multiplication (Multiplicación) Sumar grupos.

Negative numbers (Números negativos) Números menos de cero.

Numerator (Numerador) El número en la parte superior de una fracción; el numerador muestra las partes de una cantidad:

$$\frac{2}{3} = \text{numerador}$$

Operation (Operación) Suma, resta, multiplicación o división.

Ordered pair (Par ordenado) Dos números que muestran un punto en un gráfico; el primer número muestra la distancia horizontal del punto al centro del gráfico y el segundo muestra la distancia vertical del punto al centro del gráfico.

Pattern (Patrón) La repetición de un arreglo de números o cosas.

Percents (Por ciento) En una escala de 0 a 100, donde 100 equivale a la totalidad de algo, el por ciento cuantifica las partes de un todo.

Perimeter (Perímetro) La distancia *alrededor* de una figura.

Pi (Pi) La circunferencia de un círculo dividida entre su radio. Pi (que también se escribe π) es igual a 3.14.

Positive numbers (Números positivos) Números mayor que cero.

Probability (Probabilidad) Relación que muestra las posibilidades de que algo suceda:

$$1 \text{ de cada } 3 \text{ veces o } \frac{1}{3}$$

Product (Producto) El resultado de un problema de multiplicación:

$$7 \times 8 = 56$$

Pythagorean Theorem (Teorema de Pitágoras) $a^2 = b^2 + c^2$, donde b y c son los lados de un triángulo recto y a es la hipotenusa.

Quadrant (Cuadrante) En un plano de coordenadas dividido en cuatro partes, cada parte es un cuadrante.

Quotient (Cociente) El resultado de un problema de división.

Radius (Radio) Línea recta que va desde el centro de un círculo hasta cualquier punto del círculo; la mitad de un diámetro:

Range (Rango) La distancia entre el más bajo y el más alto de una serie de números.

Ration (Ratio) Comparación de dos números.

Rectangle (Rectángulo) Figura geométrica de cuatro lados y cuatro ángulos de 90 grados.

Scatterplot (Diagrama de dispersión) Un gráfico con muchos puntos. Cada punto representa un dato.

Semicircle (Semicírculo) La mitad de un círculo:

Similar shapes (Figuras similares) Figuras que no son del mismo tamaño pero que tienen los mismos ángulos y el mismo número de lados.

Sphere (Esfera) Figura geométrica que tiene la forma de una pelota.

Square (Cuadrado) Figura geométrica de cuatro lados iguales y cuatro ángulos de 90 grados.

Square number (Número cuadrado) El resultado (o producto) de multiplicar un número por sí mismo:

$$3 \times 3 = 9$$

Nueve es un número cuadrado. Puedes dibujar un número cuadrado como un cuadrado:

Straight line (Línea recta) Una línea que no se dobla (una línea recta tiene 180 grados).

Table (Tabla) Un gráfico en donde escribes información.

Triangle (Triángulo) Figura geométrica de tres lados.

Variable (Variable) Letra que sustituye a un número desconocido en una ecuación:

$$x + y = 24$$

x e y son las variables de esta ecuación.

Vertex (Vértice) El punto de unión de dos líneas que forman un ángulo.

Vertical (Vertical) Línea que forma un ángulo recto con una línea horizontal.

***x*-axis (eje *x*):** La línea horizontal de un gráfico.

***y*-axis (eje *y*):** La línea vertical de un gráfico.

Index

Algebra and Functions
Coordinate graphs, 115, 149-150
Exponents, 141
Inequalities, 8, 93-94, 102, 123, 164, 177
Number line, 79-80
Patterns, 22, 47, 91, 101, 160, 163, 173
Positive and negative numbers, 79-83, 99
    addition and subtraction, 79-80, 84-85, 99, 162, 163, 176
    division and multiplication, 81, 99, 176
Quadrants, 114-115
    x-axis, 114-115
    y-axis, 114-115
Substitute numbers for variables, 89
Square root, 147
Variables 84-86, 87-88
    adding and subtracting, 84-85
    dividing and multiplying, 87-88
    solving problems with, 6, 9, 10, 100, 101, 163, 164, 176, 177

Geometry
Angles, 128
    definition, 128
    measurement, 128, 151
    right, 128
Area, 137-142
    circle inside square, 142, 182
    circle, 141, 153, 169, 182
    rectangle, 9, 137-138, 152, 153, 182
    triangle, 139, 152, 170
Circle, 127
    area, 141
    circumference, 132-133, 152, 169, 182
    diameter, 129
    radius, 129
Circumference, 132-133, 152, 169, 182
Cube, 127
Curve, 127
Geometric shapes, 127-128, 135, 151, 152
    angle, 127, 128, 135
    measurement, 128
    circle, 127, 129, 151
    diameter, 129
    radius, 129
    quadrilaterals, 131
    rectangle, 127, 131
    square, 127, 131
    triangle, 127, 130
Perimeter, 132-134, 151, 169, 170
Pi (π), 133
Pythagorean Theorem, 10, 146-148, 154, 170, 183
    hypotenuse, 130, 147
Quadrilateral, 131
Rectangle, 127, 131
Similar Shapes, 135

Sphere, 127
Square, 127, 131
Transformations, 149-150
    reflection, 149
    rotation, 149, 154
    translation, 149, 183
Triangle, 127
    acute angle, 128
    base, 139
    height, 139
    hypotenuse, 130
    obtuse angle, 128
    Pythagorean Theorem, 146-147
    right angle, 128
    vertex, 128

Mathematical Reasoning Strategies
Checking work, 83, 95-96
Draw a solution, 96
Estimate and check, 95
Make a graph, 109, 111-113
Make a table, 23, 34, 106
Use a simpler example, 95
Work backwards, 96

Measurement
Celsius and Fahrenheit, 90
Formulas, 17, 90, 101
    area of circle inside a square, 142
    area of circle, 141
    area of rectangle, 137
    area of triangle, 139
    circumference, 132-133
    definition, 91
    Pythagorean Theorem, 146
    volume, 144
Square inches and feet, 137-139
Volume, 11, 143-144, 153, 170, 183
    cube, 144

Number Sense
Addition, 19
    decimals, 65
    fractions, 52-53, 58-59
    large numbers, 28
    signal words, 20
    signed numbers, 79, 82, 162, 163
    variables, 84
    very large numbers, 31
    whole numbers, 2, 3, 28, 31, 45, 102, 159, 162, 173
Decimals, 63
    add and subtract, 65, 77, 161, 175
    compare with fractions, 63, 77, 175
    divide, 68, 77, 78
Division, 33, 41, 46, 47, 78, 102, 159, 173
    decimals, 68
    dividend, 68
    divisor, 68
    fractions, 60

larger numbers, 41
signal words, 33
signed numbers, 81
variables, 87-88
Fractions, 49
    add and subtract, different denominators, 58-59, 76, 160, 174
    add and subtract, same denominators, 52, 75, 160, 174
    denominator, 49
    divide, 54, 60, 75, 160
    fractions, decimals, and percents, 49-78
    mixed numbers, 61
    numerator, 49
    signal words, 61
    simplifying, 61
Multiplication, 32-33, 36
    by three numbers, 39
    by two numbers, 38
    decimals, 67
    fractions, 54, 57, 75, 76, 174
    percents, 174
    signal words, 33
    signed numbers, 81-82
    simplify fractions, 61, 75, 76
    variables, 87
    whole numbers, 2, 36, 46, 159
Order of operations, 35, 89
Percents, 8, 70-72, 161, 162, 175
    find the part, percent, or whole, 71
Place value, 25
Signed numbers, 79
Subtraction, 2, 19, 45, 46, 159
    decimals, 65
    fractions with different denominators, 58
    fractions with same denominators, 52
    larger numbers, 29, 31
    signal words, 20
    variables, 84

Statistics, Data Analysis, and Probability
Graphs, 109-113
    bar, 111, 122, 165, 178
    circle, 5, 110, 123, 165, 178
    line, 7, 113-114, 125-126, 166, 168, 179, 180
    line of best fit, 112
    ordered pairs, 117
    scatterplot, 112, 124, 167, 179
Mean, Median, Mode, 6, 118-119, 126, 169, 181
Probability, 107-108
Ratios, 103-107
    solving problems with, 105, 121, 154, 164, 171, 177, 183
    writing, 8, 103, 121, 164, 177
Tables, 106

INDEX

ANSWER GRID

Print your name in the boxes. Blacken the circle under each letter.

LAST NAME										FIRST NAME								MI
A	A	A	A	A	A	A	A	A	A	A	A	A	A	A	A	A	A	A
B	B	B	B	B	B	B	B	B	B	B	B	B	B	B	B	B	B	B
C	C	C	C	C	C	C	C	C	C	C	C	C	C	C	C	C	C	C
D	D	D	D	D	D	D	D	D	D	D	D	D	D	D	D	D	D	D
E	E	E	E	E	E	E	E	E	E	E	E	E	E	E	E	E	E	E
F	F	F	F	F	F	F	F	F	F	F	F	F	F	F	F	F	F	F
G	G	G	G	G	G	G	G	G	G	G	G	G	G	G	G	G	G	G
H	H	H	H	H	H	H	H	H	H	H	H	H	H	H	H	H	H	H
I	I	I	I	I	I	I	I	I	I	I	I	I	I	I	I	I	I	I
J	J	J	J	J	J	J	J	J	J	J	J	J	J	J	J	J	J	J
K	K	K	K	K	K	K	K	K	K	K	K	K	K	K	K	K	K	K
L	L	L	L	L	L	L	L	L	L	L	L	L	L	L	L	L	L	L
M	M	M	M	M	M	M	M	M	M	M	M	M	M	M	M	M	M	M
N	N	N	N	N	N	N	N	N	N	N	N	N	N	N	N	N	N	N
O	O	O	O	O	O	O	O	O	O	O	O	O	O	O	O	O	O	O
P	P	P	P	P	P	P	P	P	P	P	P	P	P	P	P	P	P	P
Q	Q	Q	Q	Q	Q	Q	Q	Q	Q	Q	Q	Q	Q	Q	Q	Q	Q	Q
R	R	R	R	R	R	R	R	R	R	R	R	R	R	R	R	R	R	R
S	S	S	S	S	S	S	S	S	S	S	S	S	S	S	S	S	S	S
T	T	T	T	T	T	T	T	T	T	T	T	T	T	T	T	T	T	T
U	U	U	U	U	U	U	U	U	U	U	U	U	U	U	U	U	U	U
V	V	V	V	V	V	V	V	V	V	V	V	V	V	V	V	V	V	V
W	W	W	W	W	W	W	W	W	W	W	W	W	W	W	W	W	W	W
X	X	X	X	X	X	X	X	X	X	X	X	X	X	X	X	X	X	X
Y	Y	Y	Y	Y	Y	Y	Y	Y	Y	Y	Y	Y	Y	Y	Y	Y	Y	Y
Z	Z	Z	Z	Z	Z	Z	Z	Z	Z	Z	Z	Z	Z	Z	Z	Z	Z	Z

STUDENT ID NUMBER								
1	1	1	1	1	1	1	1	1
2	2	2	2	2	2	2	2	2
3	3	3	3	3	3	3	3	3
4	4	4	4	4	4	4	4	4
5	5	5	5	5	5	5	5	5
6	6	6	6	6	6	6	6	6
7	7	7	7	7	7	7	7	7
8	8	8	8	8	8	8	8	8
9	9	9	9	9	9	9	9	9

DIRECTIONS

Use a number 2 pencil.

Darken circles completely.

Examples:

Wrong
Wrong
Wrong
Right

ANSWER SHEET

1	A	B	C	D	10	A	B	C	D	19	A	B	C	D	28	A	B	C	D	37	A	B	C	D
2	A	B	C	D	11	A	B	C	D	20	A	B	C	D	29	A	B	C	D	38	A	B	C	D
3	A	B	C	D	12	A	B	C	D	21	A	B	C	D	30	A	B	C	D	39	A	B	C	D
4	A	B	C	D	13	A	B	C	D	22	A	B	C	D	31	A	B	C	D	40	A	B	C	D
5	A	B	C	D	14	A	B	C	D	23	A	B	C	D	32	A	B	C	D	41	A	B	C	D
6	A	B	C	D	15	A	B	C	D	24	A	B	C	D	33	A	B	C	D	42	A	B	C	D
7	A	B	C	D	16	A	B	C	D	25	A	B	C	D	34	A	B	C	D	43	A	B	C	D
8	A	B	C	D	17	A	B	C	D	26	A	B	C	D	35	A	B	C	D	44	A	B	C	D
9	A	B	C	D	18	A	B	C	D	27	A	B	C	D	36	A	B	C	D	45	A	B	C	D

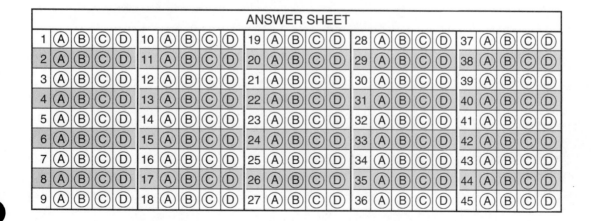

CHAPTER 2
Practice and Word Problems
Strategies 3–8
Answers and Explanations

Strategy 3, page 21

Practice A: a. 15   b. 6   c. 14   d. 12   e. 12
Practice B: a. 1   b. 6   c. 4   d. 9   e. 2   f. 4

Page 22

Practice Problems: 1. $18 - 7 = 11$ 2. $12 + 14 = 26$
Practice: The next numbers are 21 and 25. Pattern: $+1, +4, +1, +4$

Page 23

Number Fact Table for Addition and Subtraction

+/−	0	1	2	3	4	5	6	7	8	9	10
1	1	2	3	4	5	6	7	8	9	10	11
2	2	3	4	5	6	7	8	9	10	11	12
3	3	4	5	6	7	8	9	10	11	12	13
4	4	5	6	7	8	9	10	11	12	13	14
5	5	6	7	8	9	10	11	12	13	14	15
6	6	7	8	9	10	11	12	13	14	15	16
7	7	8	9	10	11	12	13	14	15	16	17
8	8	9	10	11	12	13	14	15	16	17	18
9	9	10	11	12	13	14	15	16	17	18	19
10	10	11	12	13	14	15	16	17	18	19	20

Page 24

Practice: a. 3   b. 7   c. 9   d. 13   e. 9   f. 13   g. 7   h. 6   i. 7   j. 5   k. 9   l. 9

Strategy 4, page 26

Practice:

Change	Pay
9 dimes, 10 pennies	7 dimes, 2 pennies
9 dollars, 10 dimes	3 dollars, 4 dimes
9 dollars, 9 dimes, 10 pennies	2 dollars, 7 dimes, 4 pennies

Page 27

Practice:

6 hundreds	+	13 tens	+	8 ones	=	**738**
6 hundreds	+	12 tens	+	18 ones	=	

3 hundreds	+	2 tens	+	5 ones	=	
2 hundreds	+	12 tens	+	5 ones	=	**325**
2 hundreds	+	11 tens	+	15 ones	=	

6 hundreds	+	2 tens	+	9 ones	=	
5 hundreds	+	12 tens	+	9 ones	=	**629**
5 hundreds	+	11 tens	+	19 ones	=	

Strategy 5, page 30

Practice Problems:

1. Estimate: 2:00 to 2:20 is 20 minutes.　The answer is less than 20.
   Equation: 2:21 − 2:03 =18 minutes　It is 18 minutes late.
2. Estimate: 2:00 to 2:45 is 45 minutes.　The answer is smaller than 45.
   Equation: 2:45 − 2:14 = 31 minutes　It is 31 minutes late.
3. Estimate: 3:00 to 3:58 is 58 minutes.　The answer is less than 58.
   Equation: 3:58 − 3:10 = 48 minutes　He waits 48 minutes.

Page 31

Practice Problem:

Estimate: 5000 miles + 4000 miles + 7000 miles = 16,000 miles
Equation: 4939 + 4119 + 6999 = 16,057 miles

Strategy 6, page 33

Practice:　　a. 0　　b. 40　　c. 30　　d. 18　　e. 12　　f. 0

Page 34

Number Facts Table for Multiplication and Division

×/÷	0	1	2	3	4	5	6	7	8	9	10
1	0	1	2	3	4	5	6	7	8	9	10
2	0	2	4	6	8	10	12	14	16	18	20
3	0	3	6	9	12	15	18	21	24	27	30
4	o	4	8	12	16	20	24	28	32	36	40
5	0	5	10	15	20	25	30	35	40	45	50
6	0	6	12	18	24	30	36	42	48	54	60
7	0	7	14	21	28	35	42	49	54	63	70
8	0	8	16	24	32	40	48	54	64	72	80
9	0	9	18	27	36	45	54	63	72	81	90
10	0	10	20	30	40	50	60	70	80	90	100

Page 35

Practice Problems:

1. $4 \times 6 = 24$ miles
2. boy: 30 miles ÷ 5 miles per hour = 6 hours
    bear: 30 miles ÷ 6 miles per hour = 5 hours
    $6 - 5 = 1$
    The bear gets to the island 1 hour sooner than the boy.
3. turtle: 5 hours $\times$ 5 miles per hour = 25 miles
    whale: 3 hours $\times$ 9 miles per hour = 27 miles
    $27 - 25 = 2$
    The whale swims 2 miles more than the turtle.

Practice: a. 18   b. 14   c. 27

Strategy 7, page 36

Practice: a. 852   b. 1,074   c. 3,546   d. 1,596   e. 3,136

Page 37

$5 = 500 pennies	$5 = 50 dimes
$13 = 1300 pennies	$13 = 130 dimes
$21 = 2100 pennies	$21 = 210 dimes

Practice A: a. 80   b. 66,000   c. 2,900   d. 795,000   e. 4,830   f. 56,700
Practice B:

Page 40

Practice Problems:

1. Estimate: $20 \times \$20 = \$400$ Equation: $19 \times \$17 = \$323$
2. Estimate: $20 \times 30 = 600$ Equation: $23 \times 31 = 713$ flights in January
3. Estimate: $60 \times \$30 = 1,800$ Equation: $63 \times \$26 = \$1,638$
4. Estimate: $100 \times 150 = 15,000$ Equation: $106 \times 144 = 15,264$ pens

Strategy 8, page 42

Practice: a. 224   b. 10   c. 20   d. 19   e. 30

Page 43

Practice Problems:

1. Estimate: $4000 \div 40 = 100$ Equation: $3990 \div 42 = 95$ miles a day
2. Estimate: $1200 \div 30 = 40$ Equation: $1250 \div 25 = 50$ hours
3. Estimate: $2000 \div 50 = 40$ days   Equation: $1815 \div 55 = 33$ days

CHAPTER 2
Review Test
Answers and Explanations

1. **(B)** 11 + 7 = 18 inches of snow
   The signal *plus* tells you to add.

2. **(B)** 6 − 4 = 2 pieces of gum

3. **(D)** 45 + 30 = 75 minutes
   The signal *both* tells you to add.

4. **(B)** 45 − 6 = 39 cookies
   The signal *minus* tells you to subtract.

5. **(D)** 46 + 64 = 110 points
   The signal *total* tells you to add.

6. **(B)** 115 − 48 = 67 mph
   The signal *difference* tells you to subtract.

7. **(B)** 250 − 127 = 123 words

8. **(D)** 7 × 15 = 105 minutes

9. **(A)** 45 ÷ 3 = 15
   The signal *each* tells you to divide.

10. **(D)** 6 × 8 = $48

11. **(B)** 24 ÷ 4 = 6 times a day
    The signal *per* tells you to divide.

12. **(D)** 12 × 13 = 156 donuts

13. **(B)** 1260 ÷ 420 = 3 days
    The signal *each* tells you to divide.

14. **(A)** 440 ÷ 11 = 40 hours

15. **(C)** Luis has $25 left on Friday.
    The pattern is: −10, −5, −10, −5
    The signal *How much . . . does he have left?* tells you to subtract.

Practices and Word Problems
Strategies 9–17
Answers and Explanations

Strategy 9, page 51

Practice A: a. 1/2   b. 2/6
Practice B: a. 1/4   b. 2/3   c. 4/6

Strategy 10, page 53

Practice   a. 3/3   b. 2/6   c. 4/5
Practice Problems:

1. Estimate: $3 - 1 = 2$ Equation: $\dfrac{3}{4} - \dfrac{1}{4} = \dfrac{2}{4}$ pound of ham left

2. Estimate: $1 + 2 = 3$ Equation: $\dfrac{1}{4} + \dfrac{2}{4} = \dfrac{3}{4}$ cup of frosting

3. Estimate: $4 - 1 = 3$ Equation: $\dfrac{4}{5} - \dfrac{1}{5} = \dfrac{3}{5}$ of students have balloons

Strategy 11, page 56

Practice Problems:

1. Estimate: If 2 groups = 10, there are 5 in each group.
   Equation: $\dfrac{1}{2} \times \dfrac{10}{1} = \dfrac{10}{2} = 5$ dimes

2. Estimate: If 3 groups = 9, there are 3 in each group.
   Equation: $\dfrac{1}{3} \times \dfrac{9}{1} = \dfrac{9}{3} = 3$ soft drinks

3. Estimate: If 4 groups = 8, there are 2 in each group.
   Equation: $\dfrac{1}{4} \times \dfrac{8}{1} = \dfrac{8}{4} = 2$ songs

Strategy 12, page 59

Practice Problems:

1. Estimate: $\dfrac{3}{4}$ is less than 1.   Equation: $\dfrac{3}{4} - \dfrac{1}{2} = \dfrac{3}{4} - \dfrac{2}{4} = \dfrac{1}{4}$ box of cereal

   $1 - \dfrac{1}{2} = \dfrac{1}{2}$, so

   $1 - \dfrac{3}{4}$ is less than $\dfrac{1}{2}$.

2. Estimate: $\dfrac{3}{4} - \dfrac{1}{2}$ is less than 1.   Equation: $\dfrac{3}{4} - \dfrac{1}{2} = \dfrac{3}{4} - \dfrac{2}{4} = \dfrac{1}{4}$ inch taller

3. Estimate: $\dfrac{1}{4} + \dfrac{1}{4} = \dfrac{2}{4} = \dfrac{1}{2}$ Equation: $\dfrac{1}{4} + \dfrac{1}{2} + \dfrac{1}{4} = \dfrac{1}{4} + \dfrac{2}{4} + \dfrac{1}{4} = \dfrac{4}{4} = 1$ hour

$\dfrac{1}{2} + \dfrac{1}{2} = 1$

Strategy 13, page 60

Practice Problems:

1. Estimate: Equation: $\dfrac{2}{1} \div \dfrac{1}{4} = \dfrac{2}{1} \times \dfrac{4}{1} = \dfrac{8}{1}$

   There are 8 one-fourths in 2.   8 times around the track

2. Estimate: Equation: $\dfrac{6}{8} \div \dfrac{1}{4} = \dfrac{6}{8} \times \dfrac{4}{1} =$

   There are 3 one-fourths in $\dfrac{3}{4}$. $\dfrac{24}{8} = 3$ paper strips

Page 62

Practice: a. 1/2   b. 2/3   c. $1\dfrac{1}{2}$ d. $2\dfrac{2}{3}$ e. $1\dfrac{1}{2}$

Practice Problems:

1. Estimate: $5 - 1 = 4$ Equation: $\dfrac{5}{6} - \dfrac{1}{6} = \dfrac{4}{6} = \dfrac{2}{3}$ of an inch

2. Estimate: 3 quarters + 2 quarters + 1 quarter   Equation: $\dfrac{3}{4} + \dfrac{1}{2} + \dfrac{1}{4} =$
   is more than a dollar.

   $\dfrac{3}{4} + \dfrac{2}{4} + \dfrac{1}{4} = \dfrac{5}{4} = 1\dfrac{1}{4}$ dollars

Strategy 15, page 66

Practice: a. 1.5   b. 8.90   c. 1.396   d. 81.54   e. 12.88   f. 12.577
Practice Problems:

1. Estimate: $30 + 35 + 40 = 105$ miles   Equation: $30.5 + 34.6 + 42.8 = 107.9$ miles
2. Estimate: $48 - 13 = 35$ inches   Equation: $48 - 12.56 = 35.44$ inches
3. Estimate: $116 - 110 = 6$ pounds   Equation: $116.5 - 110.3 = 6.2$ pounds

Strategy 16, page 67

Practice: a. 10.8   b. 3.15   c. 2.183   d. 24.36   e. 2.48
Practice Problem:
Estimate: $4 \times 1 = 4$ feet   Equation: $4 \times 1.3 = 5.2$ feet

Page 69

Practice Problems:

1. Estimate:
$3 \times .30 = .90$
$3 \times .15 = $ about $.40$
$+ \underline{3 \times .10 = .30}$
$ \$1.60$

    Equation: $3 \times .35 = 1.05$
$3 \times .15 = .45$
$+ \underline{3 \times .10 = .30}$
$ \$1.80$

2. Estimate:
$3 \times 4.00 = 12.00$
$3 \times 1.00 = 3.00$
$+\underline{3 \times 1.00 = 3.00}$
$ \$18.00$

    Equation: $3 \times 3.99 = 11.97$
$3 \times 1.09 = 3.27$
$+ \underline{3 \times 1.00 = 3.00}$
$ \$18.24$

3. Estimate $\$5.00 - \$1.00 = \$4.00$

    Equation: $\$5.25 - \$1.09 = \$4.16$

4. Estimate $\$2.00 \div \$5 = \$.40$

    Equation: $\$1.75 \div 5 = \$.35$
               Pancakes were .35 cents an order.

Strategy 17, page 73

Practice Problems:

1. Estimate: 50% of 45 is about 20.
         36 is more than 30.
         36 is more than 50%.

    Equation: $\dfrac{36}{45} = \dfrac{?}{100}$

    He saves 80%.

2. Estimate: $80\% = 40$

             $100\% = 50$

    Equation: $\dfrac{41}{?} = \dfrac{82}{100}$ 50 shots

3. Estimate: 10% of 125 is about 12.
         So 5% of 125 is about 6.
         The answer is between 6% and 12%.

    Equation: $\dfrac{10}{125} = \dfrac{?}{100}$

    He catches 8% of the fish in the pond.

4. Estimate: 100% is the whole thing.

         50% is half of the whole thing.
         If 6 is half, 12 is the whole.

    Equation: $\dfrac{6}{?} = \dfrac{50}{100}$
             12 cupcakes

CHAPTER 3
Review Test
Answers and Explanations

1. **(C)** $\dfrac{1}{4}$

2. **(D)** $\dfrac{4}{5}$

3. **(C)** $\dfrac{1}{4} + \dfrac{2}{4} = \dfrac{3}{4}$ of a mile

   The signal *altogether* tells you to add.

4. **(A)** $11\dfrac{5}{6} - 11\dfrac{3}{6} = \dfrac{2}{6}$ inch shorter

   The signal *shorter* tells you to subtract.

5. **(D)** $8 \div \dfrac{1}{3} = 24$ teaspoons in one stick of butter

6. **(B)** $\dfrac{1}{2} \times \dfrac{1}{2} = \dfrac{1}{4}$ of a box of brownies

7. **(A)** $\dfrac{2}{3}, \dfrac{4}{6}, \dfrac{10}{15}$

8. **(B)** $\dfrac{3}{3}$

9. **(D)** $\dfrac{1}{2} + \dfrac{1}{4} = \dfrac{2}{4} + \dfrac{1}{4} = \dfrac{3}{4}$ of a mile

   The signal *altogether* tells you to add.

10. **(C)** $5\dfrac{3}{4} - 3\dfrac{1}{4} = 2\dfrac{2}{4} = 2\dfrac{1}{2}$ hours

    The signal *how many more* tells you to subtract. Remember to simplify.

11. **(B)** $\dfrac{1}{2}$

12. **(C)** $1\dfrac{1}{4}$

13. **(B)** .3, .03, .003

14. **(B)** 3.5

15. **(C)** $22.93 + 26.66 + 26.38 + 25.36 = 101.33$ seconds

16. **(C)** $13.50 - 2.25 = 11.25$ inches

17. **(C)** $4 \times \$13.99 = \$55.96$

    The signal *altogether* tells you to add or multiply.

202   Answer Key

18. **(B)** $14.4 \div 4 = 3.6$ inches

19. **(B)** $36.6 \div 12.2 = 3$ days

20. **(D)** $25 \times 68 \div 100 = \$17.00$
    $\$68.00 - \$17.00 = \$51.00$
    The signals *percent off* tell you to find the part and then subtract.

21. **(D)** $21 \times 100 \div 35 = 60\%$ of the class gets A's

22. **(C)** $42 \times 100 \div 75 = 56$ kids are asked

23. **(C)** $48 \div 4 = 12$

24. **(B)** Change 15% to .15
    $13.60 \times .15 = \$2.04$

CHAPTER 4
Practices and Word Problems
Strategies 18–23
Answers and Explanations

Strategy 18, page 80

Word Problems:
1. Estimate: $-100 - 150 =$ more than 200 feet   Equation: $-100 - 150 = -250$ feet
2. Estimate: $+50 - 100 =$ about -50 points   Equation: $+75 - 110 = -35$ points

Page 82

Practice Problems:
1. Estimate: four 50s = 200 feet down   Equation: $4 \times -50 = -200$ feet
2. Estimate: $3 \times (-40) = -\$120$ Equation: $3 \times -\$43.25 = -\$129.75$
3. Estimate: $-50 + 25 = -25$ Equation: $-8 \times 5 = -40$;
    $ -40 + 25 = -15$
4. Estimate: $-200 \div (-20) = 10$ or more than 10   Equation: $-225 \div -15 = 15$ times

Strategy 19, page 86

Practice: a. 22 b. 14 c. 70 d. 3 e. 6.50

Practice Problems:

1. Estimate: Cost = about \$2.00 Price = about \$4.00

     \$4.00 = \$2.00 + x; about \$2.00

   Equation: \$3.75 = \$2.25 + x x = \$1.50

2. Estimate: Wettest year = this year + more rain Wettest year = about 12 inches

     This year = about 8 inches. 12 = 8 + x x is about 4

   Equation: 12.07 = 7.5 + x = 4.57 inches

3. Estimate: 6 cups of cereal = 1/2 cup of peanuts + 1/2 cup of raisins + 1/2 cup of chocolate candies + 1 cup of pretzels + y cups of cereal, 2 1/2 cups of everything else + y cups of cereal; about 4 cups

   Equation: 6 = 2 1/2 + y 6 = 3 1/2 cups of cereal

Strategy 20, page 88

Practice Problems:

1. Estimate: 150 ÷ 10 = 15   Equation: $10x = 150$; $x = 15$ sit-ups
2. Estimate: 28 ÷ 7 = 4   Equation: $7x = 28$; $x = 4$ calls each day
3. Estimate: 300 ÷ 50 = 6   Equation: $315 = 45x$; $x = 7$ classes

Strategy 22, page 94

Practice: 1. a.   2. b.   3. c.

Practice Problems: 1. b. T < 8000   2. c. $x \leq y - 3$

Strategy 23, page 97

Practice Problems:

1. 1/5 of the paintings = 12 paintings So all the paintings or 5/5 = 5 × 12 = 60 paintings

| 1/5 of the paintings or 12 to his son | 1/4 of the paintings or 15 to his neighbor | 1/3 of the paintings or 20 to a museum | He keeps 13 paintings. |

2. 120 − 45 = 75   75 − 30 = 45   45 − 20 = 25   He has 25 minutes left.

3. 40% is close to 50% or 1/2. 1/2 of 60 = 30. The answer is less than \$30.
   Use the real numbers. 40% of 59.95 = .40 × 59.95 = \$23.98 The jacket costs \$59.95 − \$23.98 = \$35.97 on sale.

4. $10 \times \dfrac{3}{4} = \dfrac{30}{4} = 7$ Use the real numbers.   10 1/2 = 21/2

   $\dfrac{3}{4} \times \dfrac{21}{2} = \dfrac{63}{8} = 7\dfrac{7}{8}$ There are 7 7/8 servings in the box.

CHAPTER 4
Review Test
Answers and Explanations

Page 99

1. **(B)** – 45 seconds

    Your goal is 7 minutes. You can run a mile in 7 minutes 45 seconds. Subtract 45 seconds from your time.

2. **(C)** -4

    Strategy: Draw a solution.

3. **(A)** $-$ 70 feet

    Strategy: Draw a solution.

4. **(B)** $+15 - 10$

5. **(D)** 48

    The parentheses tell you to multiply. Two negative signs (-12 and -4) in a multiplication problem always have a positive answer.

6. **(C)** 3

    The two negative signs (-12 and -4) in a division problem always have a positive answer.

7. **(B)** $x = \$50 - 2\,(\$5) = \$40$

    Strategy: Draw a solution.

$25 $5 off		$25 $5 off

    $+$

    $= \$40$

8. **(A)** $\$26.00 = 10x + 3x = 13x;\ x = \$2.00$

    Strategy: Draw a solution.

    1 class   1 class   1 class   1 class   1 class

9. **(D)** 220 miles Draw a solution.
220 gallons of gas Go 22 miles on 1 gallon of gas.

$$\boxed{22}\boxed{22}\boxed{22}\boxed{22}\boxed{22}$$
$$\boxed{22}\boxed{22}\boxed{22}\boxed{22}\boxed{22}$$

$\boxed{22}\boxed{22} = 220$

10. **(C)** 3 miles
Strategy: Use the map.

11. **(B)** 5 1/2
The signals $m = 5$ and $n = 3$ tell you to substitute (put in) 5 for m and 3 for n in the equation.

12. **(D)** 36
Parentheses tell you to add the x and y before you multiply by 3. The signals $x = 7$ and $y = 5$ tell you to substitute (put in) 7 for x and 5 for y in the equation.

13. **(C)** 33.33
Write your information in the formula.
Write 13 for inches.

14. **(B)** 14
Write -10 in the formula for C (Centigrade).

15. **(C)** 12
The pattern tells you to add 2 1/2 to a number to get the next number.

16. **(D)** 103
First add 10, and then 20, and then 30. Add 40 to get the 5th number in the series.

17. **(A)** $75 = 2x + 5$
Strategy: Draw a solution.

18. **(D)** $y \geq 30$ minutes

19. **(B)** {11, 12, 13, 14, . . .}

20. **(B)** $x \geq 23$ and $x \leq 64$

21. **(C)** Check multiplication by dividing.

22. **(D)** Check subtraction by adding.

CHAPTER 5
Practices and Word Problems
Strategies 24–28
Answers and Explanations

Strategy 24, page 104

Practice Problems:
1. 1:6 or 1/6
2. 23:1 or 23/1

Page 106

Practice Problems:

People with cats	People with dogs
16	18
32	36

Strategy 25, page 108

Practice Problems:
1. 1 out of 10 or 1/10 or 1:10
2. 1 out of 2 or 1/2 or 1:2
3. 10 out of 30 or 1/3 or 1:3

Strategy 26, page 109

a. data
b. conclusion
c. label
d. key
e. results

Strategy 27, page 117

Practice Problem:

x	y	Quadrant	Ordered Pair
1	-3	4	$(1, -3)$
3	-7	4	$(3, -7)$
-5	9	2	$(-5, 9)$

Strategy 28, page 119

Practice Problems:
1. Total = 25 people
2. Range = 2 people to 7 people
3. Mean or Average = the third family with 5 people
4. Mode (or the number that occurs most often) = 7 people
5. Median (or the middle number) = 5 people

Page 120

Total Fish in the Lake = 100	
Ratio of catfish to total	20:100
Ratio of bluefish to total	50:100
Ratio of yellowfish to total	30:100

1. **(A)** 2 catfish
   20 out of 100 = 2 out of 10

2. **(A)** 5 bluefish
   50 out of 100 = 5 out of 10

3. **(B)** 3 yellow fish
   30 out of 100 = 3 out of 10

4. **(A)** 1/7   1 out of 7 names

5. **(B)** 6/7   6 out of 7 names

6. **(B)** 1/6   Roseanne picks a name and
   keeps it. So there are only 6 names left.

7. **(B)** 8 students

8. **(A)** 7 students
   15 students − 8 students = 7 students

9. **(D)** 27 students
   4 + 8 + 15 = 27 students

10. **(D)** 12% of the students were born in
    South America.

11. **(D)** > the number of students from Africa

12. **(C)** 456 students   38% = .38
    .38 × 1200 = 456

13. **(C)** José, Bill

14. **(A)** Juan, Seth, Jerry

15. **(B)** 175

16. **(B)** $5.50

17. **(B)** February, March

18. **(D)** June

19. **(D)** $8.00 All of her raises are 50 cents.
    7.50 + .50 = 8.00

20. **(A)** Line A $y = 2x$ Check an x value:
    $x = 2, y = 2(2) = 4$
    Ordered pair: (2, 4)

21. **(B)** Line B $y = 3x - 4$
    Check an x value.
    $x = 2y = 3(2) - 4 = 2$
    Ordered pair: (2, 2)

22. **(C)** 165 miles
    $(105 + 320 + 130 + 105) \div 4 = 165$

23. **(A)** 105 It is the mode. It occurs two times.
    Modes occur more than any other numbers.

24. **(B)** 130 miles A median is the middle
    number.
    105   130   320

Strategies for Test-Taking Success: Math © Thomson Heinle.
Photocopying this page is prohibited by law.

CHAPTER 6
Practice and Word Problems
Strategies 31–34
Answers and Explanations

Strategy 31, page 140

Practice Problems:

1. Area of Triangle 2 = 2 × Area of
    Triangle One
    Triangle 1: Height = 2, Base = 3
    Triangle 2: Height = 4, Base = 6
    Area = 1/2 Base × Height ($A = 1/2\ bh$) =
    12 square inches

2. Find the area of each triangle. Add the areas.
    Area = 1/2 Base × Height ($A = 1/2\ bh$)
    Area of Triangle 1: Area = 1/2(4 × 3) =
    6 square centimeters
    Area of Triangle 2: Area = 1/2(3 × 2.4)
    = 3.6 square centimeters
    3.6 square centimeters + 6 square
    centimeters = 9.6 square centimeters

3. Area of rectangle = 24 square miles

    l = 8 miles

    Area = length × width ($A = lw$)
    24 = 8 × width
    width = 3 miles

4.

    width = 2 miles
    length = 3 miles

    width = .75 mile
    length = 1 mile

Length	Width	Area
3	2	6 square miles
1	.75	.75 square mile
		Total area = 6.75 square miles

Practice Problems:

1. The arm of the water sprinkler = the radius
    of the circle = 3 feet
    Use the formula:
    Area = pi × radius × radius ($A = \pi r^2$)
    A = 3.14 × 3 × 3 = 28.26 square feet

2. A radius = 1/2 × 5 inches = 2.5 inches
    Use the formula:
    Area = pi × radius × radius ($A = \pi r^2$)
    A = 3.14 × 2.5 × 2.5 = 19.625 square
    inches

3. A radius = .5 inch
    Use the formula:
    Area = pi × radius × radius ($A = \pi r^2$)
    A = 3.14 × .5 × .5 = .785 square inches

Strategy 32, Page 145

Practice Problems:

1. Use the formula:
    Volume = length × width × height
    ($V = lwh$)
    Volume = 40 × 22 × 8 = 7040 cubic feet

2. (a) Volume of the second box is twice the
    volume of the first box.
    Use the formula:
    Volume = length × width × height
    ($V = lwh$)
    First box: Volume = 15 × 8 × 2 = 240
    cubic inches
    Second box: height = 2 × 2 = 4
    Second box: Volume = 15 × 8 × 4 = 480
    cubic inches

Strategy 33, Page 148

Practice Problems:

1. Use the Pythagorean Theorem: $A^2 = B^2 + C^2$
   The distance across the park $= A$
   $.4^2 + .3^2 = A^2 = .25$
   The square root of $.25 = .5$
   The distance across the park is .5 mile.
   $.4 + .3 = .7 =$ the distance around the park
   $.7 - .5 = .2$ mile farther around the park
   than across the park

2. Use the Pythagorean Theorem: $A^2 = B^2 + C^2$
   $B = 5 \quad C = 12$
   $A^2 = 5^2 + 12^2$
   $A^2 = 25 + 144$
   $A^2 = 169$
   $A = 13$
   The airplane flies 13 feet.

3. Use the Pythagorean Theorem: $A^2 = B^2 + C^2$
   $B = .4 \quad A = .5$
   $.5^2 = .4^2 + C^2$
   $.5^2 - .4^2 = C^2 \quad .25 - .16 = C^2$
   $C^2 = 9 \quad 3 \times 3 = 9 \quad C = 3$
   Mr. Greylock drives .4 of a mile $+$ .3 of a
   mile $=$ .7 of a mile

CHAPTER 6
Review Test
Answers and Explanations

Pages 151–154

1. A. circle B. square C. triangle

2. D. side E. right angle F. vertex

3. G. radius H. circumference I. diameter

4. A. 360 B. 180 C. 90

5. **(B)** 11 inches
The perimeter is the distance around a figure.
3 inches + 5 inches + 3 inches = 11 inches

6. **(C)** 18.84 centimeters
Use the formula:
Circumference = pi × diameter
$C = 2\pi r$ $C = 2\pi 3$ $C = 2 \times 3.14 \times 6 =$ 18.84 centimeters

7. **(D)** 14 feet
Andros needs to cut the perimeter of the window. The perimeter is 3 + 4 + 3 + 4.

8. **(C)** Use the formula:
Area = length × width $(A = lw)$
Area = 90 × 80 = 7200 square feet

9. **(C)** Triangles A, B, C
Similar figures must have equal angles.
All the triangles have equal angles even though their sides are different lengths.

10. **(B)** 4 square feet
Use the formula: Area = 1/2 base × height
$A = 1/2\ bh$
$A = 1/2 \times 4 \times 2$
$A = 4$ square feet
Remember to give area in square feet.

11. **(D)** 40 square inches
Use the formula: Area = length × width
$A = lw$
$A = 8 \times 5$
$A = 40$ square inches
Remember to give area in square inches.

12. **(C)** 14 square meters.

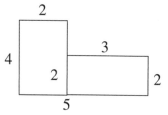

Separate the figure into two rectangles.
Find the area for each rectangle.
The area for the first rectangle is 8 square meters.
The area for the second rectangle is 6 square meters.
Add the areas together to get 14 square meters total area.

13. **(D)** 50.24 square centimeters
Use the formula: $A = \pi r^2$
Area = pi × radius squared
Area = $3.14 \times 4^2 = 3.14 \times 16 = 50.24$

14. **(D)** 40.5 cubic inches
Use the formula:
Volume = length × width × height
$V = lwh$
$V = 4.5 \times 1.5 \times 6$
$V = 40.5$ cubic inches
Remember to give the volume in cubic inches.

15. **(B)** 17 feet
Use the formula:
$$A^2 + B^2 = C^2$$
$$8^2 + 15^2 = C^2$$
$$64 + 225 = C^2$$
$$\sqrt{289} = \sqrt{C^2}$$
$$17 = C$$

16. **(A)** Rotation
The figure has turned around about 30°.
It is called rotation when a figure turns around.

17. **(B)** 2.25 meters
The ratio of the sides of the two rectangles is 1.5 to 1.
EG = 1.5 × AC
EG = 1.5 × 1.5
Because the opposite sides of rectangles are equal, EF is also 2.25 meters.

CHAPTER 7

Cumulative Practice Test 1
Answers and Explanations

Pages 155–183

1. (C) 10 pairs
The signal *altogether* tells you to add.

2. (D) 60 tickets
Look at the question: How many tickets does the team give out?
Team means all the girls.
Each girl has 4 tickets.
We are adding 15 groups of 4.
Multiplication is the quick way to add groups.
Multiply: 15 × 4

3. (B) 960 minutes
Two parts make a whole. Subtract to find one part.
Minutes Greg sleeps + minutes Greg is awake = total minutes in a day
Total minutes in a day − minutes Greg sleeps = minutes Greg is awake

4. (C) 1815 pennies
The two parts together make the total.
Add to combine the parts.
1248 pennies + 567 pennies = total pennies

5. (A) 25 rows
The chairs are in groups of 20.
We need to find out how many of these groups are in 500.
Division is a quick way to find how many groups are in a total.
Divide: 500 ÷ 20

6. (C) 20 miles
Look for the pattern.
Each day Luan walks + 2 miles more each day.

7. (B) 1/2 cup of raisins
Two parts make a total.
Subtract to find one part. Don't forget to simplify your answer.

Subtract: $\dfrac{3}{4} - \dfrac{1}{4} = \dfrac{2}{4} = \dfrac{1}{2}$

8. (B) 1 2/3 feet of wood
Frank has 5 pieces of wood. Each piece is 1/3 of a foot long.
He wants to add all the pieces.
Multiplication is a quick way to add all the pieces.
Don't forget to simplify your answer.
Multiply: 5 × 1/3 = 5/3 = 1 2/3

9. (D) 6 minutes
The two parts together make the total.
Add to combine the parts.
Don't forget to simplify your answer.
Add: 3 1/2 + 2 1/2 = 5 2/2 = 6

10. (B) 3/4 of an hour
The signal *altogether* tells you to add.
Remember you can only add things that are the same.
Change the quarter and the half to quarters.
Then add: 1/4 + 2/4 = 3/4

11. (C) 34 lines
Divide to find how many 1/4 inches are in 8 1/2 inches.
Remember to change 8 1/2 to 17/2 before you divide. Then invert the second fraction and multiply.

$$\frac{17}{2} \div \frac{1}{4} = \frac{17}{2} \times \frac{4}{1} = \frac{68}{2} = 34$$

12. (D) 1500 dogs and cats

Add the percentages to find what percent of people own dogs and cats.

Then you need to use the percent to find the number of dogs and cats.

Multiply: $2000 \times .75 = 1500$

13. (B) 48 students

Look at the table. Look at the total number of students.

Look at the percent of students that like each color.

Use the percent to find the number of students that like each color.

Multiply: $.40 \times 120 = 48$

14. (B) .05 of the students

The signal *How many more* tells you to subtract.

Subtract the students who like the other colors from the students who like blue.

Subtract: $.40 - .35 = .05$

15. (A) .25 of the students

Add all the students in the table.

Subtract from 100.

Subtract: $100 - .75 = .25$

16. (B) between 25% and 30% of the earth is dry land.

100% is the total.

Subtract the part.

Subtract: $100\% - 75\% = 25\%$ and $100\% - 70\% = 30\%$

17. (D) 75% of the questions are correct.

$$\frac{part}{hundred} = \frac{part}{whole} \qquad \frac{63}{84} = \frac{?}{100}$$

$6300 \div 84 = 75$

18. (D) 560 seniors

$$\frac{part}{hundred} = \frac{part}{whole} \qquad \frac{448}{?} = \frac{80}{100}$$

$44800 \div 80 = 560$

19. (C) $114.00

Subtract total negative numbers from total positive numbers.

$+\$159.00 - \$45.00 = \$114.00$

20. (A) $-40°$ F

The signal *8 times colder* tells you to multiply.

$-5 \times 8 = -40$

21. (B) $- 13°$

Increasing negative numbers means they become less negative.

To increase 3° from $-16°$ means to be 3° less negative.

$-16° + 3° = -13°$

22. (B) 145 pounds

Look at the pattern.

Strategy: Make a table.

He weighs 150 pounds now.	
Lose 2 pounds, gain 1 pound every week.	
First week	$150 - 2 + 1 = 149$
Second week	$149 - 2 + 1 = 148$
Third week	$148 - 2 + 1 = 147$
Fourth week	$147 - 2 + 1 = 146$
Fifth week	**$146 - 2 + 1 = 145$**

23. (C) Blue jeans: $21.40; Gym shoes: $80.25

Use the equation: $x + .07x = cost$

Substitute a price for x.

24. (D) $2.50x + .50(x - 30)$

Think: Total boxes of candy times $2.50 then subtract 30 boxes. Multiply your answer by .50.

25. (A) $50 \div x =$ number of candy bars

Think: total number of candy bars separated into groups

Divide 50 by the number of girls.

26. (B) $\{81, 82, \ldots, 89, 90\}$

Remember: $>$ means more than a number.

$\le$ means less than or equal to a number.

27. (C) Gwen and Mary

Ali cannot take the medicine because he $= 6$. He is not > 6. Charlie cannot take the medicine because he $= 5$. He is not > 6.

28. (A) 1:2

1:2 is another way of writing "one out of two."

Strategies for Test-Taking Success: Math © Thomson Heinle. Photocopying this page is prohibited by law.

29. (C) 25 out of 73
To select a probability, think of *possible* choices out of *total* choices.

30. (A) Boys age 0 to 5
Look at the bar graph.
The longest bar is for "Boys age 0 to 5"

31. (A) 2.5%
Look at the circle graph.
Only 4 children out of 160 are allergic to peanuts.
Find: 4 = what percent of 160

$$\frac{part}{hundred} = \frac{part}{whole} \qquad \frac{4}{160} = \frac{?}{100}$$

$$400 \div 160 = 2.5$$

32. (B) The weight of the car affects how many miles a car drives on a gallon of gas.
Look at the graph.
Use only the information on the graph to get your answer. The graph does not show *all* heavy cars.

33. (A) January
Look at the graph.
Look at the differences between the lowest and highest temperatures each month.

34. (C) (4,10)
Use the equation of the line in the problem:
$y = 4x - 6$
Substitute 4 for *x*. Solve. Use the *y*-value for the ordered pair. Don't forget order of operations.
$y = 4 \times 4 - 6 \ y = 10$

35. (A) 80
The mode is the most frequent number in the list.

36. (C) 88
The mean is the average number in the list.
Add the list together and divide by the number of tests.

$82 + 80 + 83 + 80 + 94 + 97 + 100 =$
$616 \div 7 = 88$

37. (B) 83
List the numbers in order from smallest to largest.
The median is the middle number.

38. (B) 39.25 inches
Use the formula: $C = \pi d$
Use 3.14 for π. Use 12.5 for *d*.
$C = 3.14 \times 12.5 = 39.25$

39. (C) 122.66 square inches
Remember: the radius is 1/2 the diameter.
Use the formula: $A = \pi r^2$. Use 3.14 for π. Use 6.25 for *r*.
$3.14 \times 6.25 \times 6.25 = 122.65625 = 122.66$

40. (C) Perimeter
You want to find the distance around the baseball field.
Perimeter is the distance around.

41. (A) 60 square feet
Use the formula: $A = 1/2 \ bh$
Substitute 15 for *b* and 8 for *h*.

42. (B) 40 feet
Perimeter is the distance around the figure.
$8 + 15 + 17 = 40$

43. (D) 160 cubic inches of ice cream
Use the formula: $V = lwh$
Substitute 8 for length, 5 for width, and 4 for height.
$V = 8 \times 5 \times 4 = 160$

44. (C) 5 feet
Use the Pythagorean Theorem:
$$A^2 = B^2 + C^2$$
$$13^2 = 12^2 + C^2$$
$$169 = 144 + C^2$$
$$169 - 144 = C^2$$
$$125 = C^2$$
$$5 = C$$

45. (C) 10 miles
The ratio of the sides of the similar triangles is 3 to 2.
15 to 10 = 3 to 2

**Cumulative Practice Test 2
Answers and Explanations**

Pages 173–183

1. (C) 66¢
Add when you put a group of things together.
25 + 25 + 10 + 5 + 1 = 66

2. (A) 241 days
Take away not-working days from Jack's total workdays.
Take away weekend and vacation days and holidays.
365 − 104 − 10 − 10 = 241

3. (B) 25 feet
The signal *how much taller* tells you to subtract.
4418 − 4398 = 25

4. (A) 25 rows
Divide the whole number into equal groups.
1000 ÷ 40 = 25

5. (B) 6 rows
Strategy: Draw a picture.

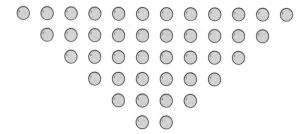

6. (B) 1/2 inch
Subtract Suzy's height in September from Suzy's height today.
Don't forget to simply the fraction.
5 3/4 − 5 1/4 = 2/4 = 1/2

7. (D) 8 ears
Suzy's parents buy corn for the family altogether. Add all the ears of corn.
1 1/2 + 2 + 2 1/2 + 1 + 1 = 7 2/2 = 8

8. (B) 36 pages
Gabriel reads two out of three parts of his book. Multiply 54 pages by 2/3.
$$\frac{2}{3} = 54 = \frac{108}{3} = 36$$

9. (B) 5/6 of a can
First change all the amounts of oil to sixths.
1/2 = 3/6 1/3 = 2/6
Then add all the oil in all the cans.
3/6 + 2/6 = 5/6

10. (C) 72 cones
Divide to find how many 2/3 of a cup are in 48 cups.
$$48 \div \frac{2}{3} = 48 \times \frac{3}{2} = \frac{144}{2} = 72$$

11. (B) 6600 people
Estimate: 55% is about half of 12,000. Half of 12000 is 6000. So 6600 is probably the right answer. Multiply to check:
.55 × 12000 = 6600

12. (A) 2 of the juices
.50 is half. Only Sun Orange Juice and White Grape Juice are more than .50.

13. (C) .75 more real juice
The signal *how much more* tells you to subtract.
.90 − .15 = .75

14. (D) .65 sugar water
1.00 = the whole amount
So 1.00 − .35 = .65 sugar water

15. (D) 12 tablespoons oil
Strategy: Look for the pattern. Make a table.

Vinegar	Oil
1	2
2	4
3	6
4	8
5	10
6	12

16. (D) 40% of the time
Estimate: Half of 30 days is 15 days.
12 is a little less than half.
40% is probably the answer.
Multiply to check: $.40 \times 30 = 12$

17. (B) 26 cars
Remember to change 65% to .65. Then multiply.
$.65 \times 40 = 26$

18. (D) +55 points
Add all the +s: 25
Add 25 points to Alison's points at the beginning of the year. $25 + 50 = 75$
Add all the −s: −20
Combine the −s and the +s:
$75 + (-20) = 55$ points

19. (D) −150 feet
Multiply groups: $5 (-30) = -150$

20. (B) 9 pieces, 2/3 of a foot each
Strategy: Draw a picture.

1 piece
_____

3 pieces
_____ _____ _____

9 pieces
___ ___ ___ ___ ___ ___ ___ ___ ___

Only one answer has the correct number of pieces, 9. To find the length of each piece, divide 6 (the length) by 9 (number of pieces).
$$\frac{6}{9} = \frac{2}{3}$$

21. (D) $27.14
Estimate: the cost of the dinner + the tip is more than the cost of the dinner alone.
Solve the equation:
$x + .15x = \$23.60 + .15(23.60) = \$27.14$

22. (B) 10° Celsius

Do the equation: Celsius $= (50 - 32) \times \dfrac{5}{9}$
$$\text{Celsius} = 18 \times \frac{5}{9}$$
$$\text{Celsius} = 10°$$

23. (A) .55h
Strategy: Guess and check.
If the boy is 6 feet when he grows up:
A. $.55 \times 6 = 3.3$ feet
B. $6 + .55 = 6.55$
C. $6 + 5.5 = 11.5$
D. $6 \div .55 = 10.9$
The closest answer is .55 h.

24. (A) $50 \div x =$ number of pencils
Mr. Rodriquez puts the 50 pencils in groups. He gives a group to each student. He divides the pencils.

25. (B) {28, 29, . . . , 31}
Remember that $\geq$ and $\leq$ include the beginning and ending numbers.

26. (D) only Charles
The sign says that children ≤ 12 cannot visit without a parent. This means that children $= 12$ and < 12 cannot visit alone. This means only 13-year-old-Charles can visit without a parent.

27. (B) 8:10
Ratios are part compared to whole.

28. (B) 1 out of 15
Add all the prizes: $200 + 100 + 50 + 25 = 375$ prizes
25 prizes out of 375 prizes will be cars.
$$\frac{25}{375} = \frac{1}{15}$$

29. (C) 5000 tigers
Look at the bar on the chart.
Tigers are gray. The gray bar stops at 5000.

30. (A) About 8:1
There are 140 pandas living outside of zoos and 1100 tigers. 1100/140 is close to 8/1.

Strategies for Test-Taking Success: Math © Thomson Heinle.
Photocopying this page is prohibited by law.

31. (A) 29.5 seconds

The fastest time will be the lowest number. It only takes Raj 29.5 seconds to swim the 50-yard freestyle.

32. (B) 30 km/hr

The signal *difference* tells you to subtract.

$110 - 80 = 30$

33. (B) (4, 7)

Substitute 4 for x.

$y = 3x - 5$

$y = 3(4) - 5$

$y = 12 - 5$

$y = 7$

34. (C) -3

The mean is the average temperature. Add all the temperatures.

Divide the total by the number of temperatures.

35. (B) -5

The median is the middle temperature.

Write the temperatures from the smallest to the largest.

Find the temperature in the middle.

36. (B) -5

The mode is the most frequent temperature. Jan. 6, 11, and 13 are $-5°$.

All the other temperatures happen once or twice.

37. (C) 47.1 inches

Substitute the diameter into the formula.

$C = \pi d \quad C = 3.14 \times 15$

38. (C) 314 square feet

Use the formula: $A = \pi r^2$

Remember that radius $= 1/2(d)$. The diameter is 20. The radius $= 10$.

$A = 3.14 (10) (10)$

$A = 314$

39. (A) The first bedroom

Area measures bedroom size.

The formula for area is: $A = lw$

Bedroom 1: $10 \times 11 = 110$ sq. ft.

Bedroom 2: $9 \times 12 = 108$ sq. ft.

Bedroom 3: $10 \times 10 = 100$ sq. ft.

40. (B) 24 square feet

Use the formula for area of a triangle:

$A = 1/2 \, bh$

Substitute the numbers from the triangle:

$A = 1/2 (6) (8)$

41. (B) 200.96 square inches

Half the side of the square is a radius of the circle. Half the side is 8 inches.

The formula for the area of a circle: $A = \pi r^2$

$A = 3.14 (8) (8)$

42. (C) 48 cubic feet of stones

Use the formula for volume: $V = lwh$

Substitute the numbers for the space under the porch.

$V = 8 (12) (.5)$

43. (B) 5 feet

Use the Pythagorean Theorem:

$A^2 = B^2 + C^2$

Substitute the numbers for the sides of the triangle:

$A^2 = (3) (3) + (4) (4) = 25$

Find the square root of 25. This is the number multiplied by itself makes 25.

$5 \times 5 = 25$

44. (C) 12 inches wide

Use the idea of similar figures.

The ratio of the sides of the small cookie sheet equals the ratio of the sides of the big cookie sheet.

$\dfrac{8}{14} = \dfrac{4}{7} = \dfrac{x}{21}$

$3 \times 7 = 21$ and $3 \times 4 = 12$

45. (C) Translation

The figure "slid" across quadrants. This is called translation.